First-Time Recipes With Cast Iron Skillet

Mariamab A. Martin

All rights reserved. Copyright © 2023 Mariamab A. Martin

COPYRIGHT © 2023 Mariamab A. Martin

All rights reserved.

No part of this book must be reproduced, stored in a retrieval system, or shared by any means, electronic, mechanical, photocopying, recording, or otherwise, without written permission from the publisher.

Every precaution has been taken in the preparation of this book; still the publisher and author assume no responsibility for errors or omissions. Nor do they assume any liability for damages resulting from the use of the information contained herein.

Legal Notice:

This book is copyright protected and is only meant for your individual use. You are not allowed to amend, distribute, sell, use, quote or paraphrase any of its part without the written consent of the author or publisher.

Introduction

This is a comprehensive guide designed to help those new to cooking with cast-iron skillets unlock their culinary potential. This cookbook offers valuable insights and a wide range of recipes, making it an ideal resource for beginners in the world of cast-iron cooking.

The cookbook begins by introducing readers to the cast-iron skillet, often referred to as the mightiest skillet in the kitchen. It emphasizes the durability, versatility, and unique cooking properties of cast iron, setting the stage for readers to explore the world of cast-iron cooking.

Understanding how to make the most of a cast-iron skillet is a key focus of the guide. It provides essential tips and techniques for seasoning, cleaning, and maintaining the skillet to ensure it becomes a reliable kitchen companion for years to come.

One of the standout features of this cookbook is its diverse range of recipes, categorized into various sections. For breakfast and brunch lovers, there are savory and sweet options that make great use of the skillet's capabilities.

The section on bread offers recipes that highlight the skillet's ability to create perfectly baked bread, with a focus on simplicity and delicious flavors.

Skillet sides provide a selection of vegetable-focused dishes that showcase how the skillet can enhance the flavors and textures of various ingredients.

Vegetarian meals offer a variety of meat-free options, proving that cast-iron cooking is not limited to meat-centric dishes. These recipes are flavorful and satisfying, appealing to both vegetarians and omnivores alike.

Seafood and poultry recipes cater to those who enjoy the delicate flavors of seafood or the heartiness of poultry. The skillet's even heating and versatility shine in these dishes.

For meat lovers, the cookbook offers a selection of recipes that demonstrate how cast iron can be used to prepare delicious and succulent meat-based dishes.

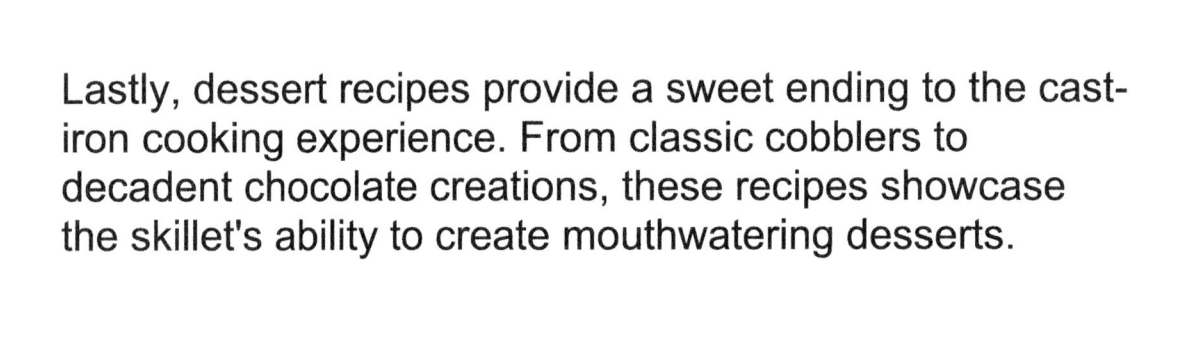

Lastly, dessert recipes provide a sweet ending to the cast-iron cooking experience. From classic cobblers to decadent chocolate creations, these recipes showcase the skillet's ability to create mouthwatering desserts.

In summary, this book introduces readers to the world of cast-iron cooking and empowers them to explore its full potential. With detailed instructions and a wide array of recipes, this cookbook is an excellent resource for individuals looking to start their culinary journey with cast iron or those seeking to expand their repertoire of cast-iron skillet recipes. Whether you're a novice cook or an experienced chef, this guide offers something for everyone to enjoy the pleasures of cooking with cast iron.

Contents

CHAPTER 1: Getting to Know Your Cast-Iron Skillet 1

The Mightiest Skillet of Them All 2

How to Unlock the Power of Your Cast-IronSkillet 8

Cast-Iron Companions 13

How to Use This Book 14

CHAPTER 2: Breakfast and Brunch 17

CHAPTER 3: Breads 63

CHAPTER 4: Skillet Sides 89

CHAPTER 5: Vegetarian Meals 118

CHAPTER 6: Seafood and Poultry 153

CHAPTER 7: Meat 185

CHAPTER 8: Dessert 218

CHAPTER 1: Getting to Know Your Cast-Iron Skillet

My favorite gift for newlyweds is a 12" cast-iron skillet because it's the ideal starter piece—a simple way for new users to get comfortable. I also love to use cast iron as an allegory for marriage: If you nurture it and give it care and attention when needed, it will last a lifetime.

The Mightiest Skillet of Them All

For many, cast iron conjures up images of a Southern grandma cooking at her stove, or a troop of Scouts putting together a rustic campfire dinner. And although both can absolutely be true, cast iron is beloved by all kinds of home cooks and professional chefs around the world. Here's why.

Versatility: My 12" skillet never leaves our stovetop because it's the most versatile tool in our kitchen. It is thick enough for frying, it conducts and retains heat evenly for sautéing, and it easily moves from the stove to the oven for roasting and baking. You can even put it directly over the flames of a grill or campfire, which makes it our go-to pan year-round.

Durability: Although it's not impossible to damage a skillet beyond repair, it's darn near close. It is made of iron. It's sturdy and can handle pretty much anything you can throw at it. Better yet, almost everything can be fixed with a nice, deep clean and seasoning.

Value: Cast iron is inexpensive, but it isn't cheap. A new, ready-to-use skillet costs around $30 and is of such good quality that you'll be able to pass it on to your grandchildren. And that's for a new skillet! Plenty of cast iron can be picked up for a bigger bargain at thrift stores and yard sales. You'll rarely find a skillet that a little elbow grease can't fix.

Sustainability: Over time, many other types of cookware will chip or become damaged in a way that makes them either toxic or unusable, meaning they must be thrown away and replaced. Cast iron is naturally nonstick, and its production doesn't create any hazardous byproducts that end up in our waterways. Cleaned and reseasoned without any harsh chemicals, a gently maintained skillet can last for generations.

Longevity: The pride and joy of my family's collection is a 40-quart cauldron that my great-grandmother Sybil inherited from someone further up her family tree. In my regular rotation, I have cast-iron pieces that belonged to my grandmother and my father, and I imagine that these pieces, along with others I've collected, will be in perfect condition to pass on to my children. The key to successfully keeping cast iron in good condition for generations is seasoning. More on that later.

My Five Favorite Foods to Cook in Cast Iron

Every chef has favorite recipes, dishes they simply can't—or won't—make without their trusty cast-iron skillet. Here are five of mine.

FRIED EGGS: I inherited my father's love of fried eggs—as well as his finicky opinions about them. I could eat a fried egg every day, but I believe that the very best comes from a quick fry in a well-seasoned skillet with a pat of butter. See the Skillet Eggs and Bacon recipe.

STEAK: Cooking steak can be intimidating. It's a pricey cut of meat that, when overcooked or undercooked, can easily be ruined. That said, there's no better steak than one that is seared in a hot skillet. See the Perfect Cast-Iron Steak recipe.

HUEVOS RANCHEROS: This is a family favorite! A tortilla, cheese, and an egg come together seamlessly on a skillet's nonstick surface, making the rather tricky task of flipping over the tortilla easy as can be. See the Huevos Rancheros recipe.

CORNBREAD: In the fall and winter, homemade chili is in constant rotation, and no chili dinner is complete without cornbread. Skillet cornbread has the benefit of all crisp edges and a moist center. See the Masa Harina Cornbread recipe.

VINEGAR PIE: I love how it feels to walk into a party carrying a skillet full of creamy pie. It's a showstopper, and not just because it's full of sugar and spices. A pie baked in a skillet will never have a soggy bottom; each slice is crisp crust and silky center. See the Vinegar Pie recipe.

What Is Seasoning?

A word you'll hear over and over when talking about cast iron (and a word I've already used repeatedly) is seasoning. For many people this sounds intimidating and can scare them off cast iron, thinking it's too finicky. Let's demystify this important element of cast-iron care.

Seasoning is a layer of fat that has polymerized and bonded with the iron. This protects the iron and gives it a beautiful shine and luster. Seasoning is built up over time, but it can also be damaged. Thankfully, damage can be avoided through regular care and maintenance, and it can be repaired through reseasoning. A well-seasoned skillet has a smooth, oiled surface that is durable and naturally nonstick. Once a skillet has been well seasoned, it will be pitch black with a natural, slick patina and a soft shine that is easy to maintain through regular care and cleaning. You will occasionally need to reseason your skillet, which is as simple as cleaning and re-oiling it a few times to restore its patina.

The more you use your skillet, the more comfortable you will be maintaining the seasoning and knowing how different dishes affect it. Foods cooked with lots of fat or oil—frying, cooking bacon, searing meat—help build the seasoning, while foods that are acidic or moist—tomatoes, stewed beans—strip away the seasoning. All these dishes are wonderful when made in cast iron, but how you treat your skillet after cooking them will impact how the seasoning is maintained.

How to Season Your Cast Iron

When you buy a skillet new, it will come advertised as "preseasoned"—but don't let that fool you. You'll still want to season it yourself to ensure that it is truly nonstick. The following instructions work for both a new, preseasoned skillet and a freshly stripped older skillet.

1. Pour ½ cup of coarse sea salt into your skillet and give it a good scr towel. This will take care of any grime that has built up on its journey kitchen.

2. Wash it with mild dish soap and hot water.

3. Place it on the stove over medium heat until it is completely dry.

4. Coat the skillet (warm from the stovetop) with oil, such as vegetable, coconut, or peanut. Start with about 1 tablespoon and spread it arou clean rag, using more as needed to coat it thoroughly on the top, bo sides, and handle. Drain off any excess.

5. Preheat the oven to 450°F. Place the cast iron in the oven for 30 min Turn off the heat and let it cool completely in the oven. Repeat this p oiling and baking three or four times until the skillet is pitch black an

Reseasoning Your Cast Iron

Occasionally you'll notice that even your most loved pieces of cast iron need to be reseasoned. It may be that you notice a chink in the seasoning, a bit of rust, or a dry spot in the patina. None of these are difficult to overcome, and you'll find the process of reseasoning similar to the initial seasoning you did on your pan.

- ☐ The first step in reseasoning depends on the damage. If what you are noticing is a rust spot, you need to scrub it out with steel wool and, in extreme cases, sandpaper. Once the rust has been worked out of the pan, follow the same steps as your initial seasoning.

- ☐ Even the most skilled chefs occasionally burn what they're cooking and leave themselves a mess of a skillet. My worst offense was forgetting a pan full of chorizo on the stove while distracted during my first pregnancy, which left my beloved 8" skillet in desperate need of a full remodel. In these instances, your approach is similar to a rust situation: Use steel wool followed by sandpaper to grind out the burn damage and then rebuild the seasoning.

- ☐ For heavily damaged pans, my father swore by an electric sander, which takes the skillet all the way back to its silver state. This is effective in quickly stripping away the damage, but the process of rebuilding the seasoning is lengthy.

- ☐ For a skillet that has been fully stripped, you will need to alternate oiling and baking and cooking with the skillet. Over time, the patina will become darker and darker until a true seasoning is achieved.

- ☐ If the need for reseasoning is a dry spot, simply give the skillet a good scrub and follow the process of re-oiling and baking three or four times.

- ☐ For general use (with no dramatic incidents), it's helpful to reseason your cast iron one or two times a year to keep the seasoning thick and healthy.

Great Moments in Cast-Iron History

Cast iron has a long and storied history, stretching through generations and across cultures.

- ☐ The earliest known cast-iron artifacts are from China and date back to the fifth century BCE.

- ☐ Its original purpose was to be poured into molds to make plowshares, pots, weapons, and pagodas.

- ☐ In Western cultures, cast iron began popping up in the fifteenth century in the form of cannons and shot.

- ☐ In 1707, Abraham Darby patented the sand-casting method, which is similar to how cast iron is made today.

- ☐ By the late 1770s, cast iron was being used for structural purposes. Through the industrial revolution, cast-iron bridges became common in Western countries.

- ☐ Lewis and Clark brought a cast-iron Dutch oven (as well as eight brass kettles) on their expedition across the Louisiana Territory in 1804.

- ☐ Cast-iron cauldrons, like the one passed down through my family, were originally used both as laundry kettles and for making large amounts of soup and stew.

- ☐ The largest collection of cast iron in the United States can be found outside Tacoma, Washington, at the Cast Iron Museum. Its owners, Larry and Marg O'Neil, built the museum to showcase some of their personal collection of 13,000 pieces.

How to Unlock the Power of Your Cast-Iron Skillet

There are as many opinions about using and cleaning your skillet as there are people who want to share them, so I'll lay out the methods I was taught by my father and grandmother. They have worked well for me over years of daily cast-iron use.

Using Your Skillet

Now that you've brought your skillet home and seasoned it thoroughly, you're ready to put it to good use. Its maiden voyage is a big moment! What will you cook first?

When I am introducing a new skillet to my collection, I try to begin with foods that will add to the seasoning, foods that are cooked in oils and fats. I like to christen a skillet with bacon. As you get comfortable with your pan, you can try different cooking methods—searing, sautéing, baking, deep-frying, and panfrying.

There are common threads running through all the recipes in this book. They highlight the same reasons people choose cast iron: It is heavy enough to withstand high temperatures, it is naturally nonstick, and it retains heat beautifully. Each recipe allows the strength and versatility of the skillet to shine.

When panfrying and deep-frying, you'll appreciate that cast iron is heavy enough to tolerate the high temperatures, and it retains the heat well. Panfrying, which is the process of frying in ¼" of oil, is ideal for patties or lightly breaded meats like Crab Cakes or Chicken Piccata. Deep-frying, which is the process of frying in 1" or more of oil, is ideal for larger pieces of meat like Nashville Hot Chicken, or soft and light dough like Churros. For sautéing and searing, that beautiful patina makes the skillet nonstick. With just a little bit of oil, the skillet is ideal for Chicken and Broccoli Stir-Fry or Perfect Cast-Iron Steak. The heft and heat retention also make it wonderful for baking everything from Masa Harina Cornbread to Apple Pie.

As you dive into the recipes in this book, you'll get a clear idea of how to use the skillet and where it really shines.

Cleaning Your Skillet

Each different method of cooking will react with a skillet's seasoning in a different way, which means you may need to adjust your approach to care after each dish. With the exception of reseasoning, I don't use soap in my cast iron. After each use I wash it with hot water and scrub it with a bristle brush or nonmetal scouring pad. The oil in the seasoning forms a polymer coating that keeps it free of harmful bacteria. Keeping the seasoning intact keeps the pan in good condition and ready for use.

When I cook foods that leave a residue of oil or fat in the pan, I allow the skillet to cool with the fat in it so that it can be absorbed into the seasoning. After the pan cools, I drain off any excess oil before cleaning. When I cook with acidic foods, or stew or braise in my skillet, it's important to clean the pan immediately after cooking and reseason before rust can develop. If the food I've been cooking is particularly messy or has left bits stuck to the surface, I'll use salt and hot water to scrub it out, since salt is coarse but will not damage the seasoning.

Once you've fully scoured your skillet with hot water, place it on the stovetop over low heat until it dries completely. It's important to dry all the water out of your skillet as quickly as possible to keep rust away. When it is dry, coat it with a thin layer of vegetable oil before storing.

Cast Iron Dos and Don'ts

Cast iron has different rules than other cookware. It has the reputation of being finicky and hard to manage, which I think makes it seem like more of a diva than it actually is. Just follow these simple rules.

Do:

- ☐ Always use a pot holder
- ☐ Heat before adding fat or oil
- ☐ Let the food sit and caramelize; moving it around can cause sticking
- ☐ Clean it immediately after use, every time
- ☐ Dry it completely after cleaning, every time
- ☐ Keep it completely oiled

Don't:

- ☐ Use harsh or abrasive cleaners; cast iron is porous, so don't put anything in your skillet that you wouldn't want on your eggs
- ☐ Allow food to sit in it overnight
- ☐ Soak it in water or use it to boil water
- ☐ Leave it to air dry overnight
- ☐ Scrape at it with metal utensils

☐ Run it through the dishwasher

Cast-Iron Companions

As you've no doubt surmised by this point, the number-one goal when working with cast iron is building up and protecting the seasoning. There are, however, some tools that will make your relationship with your skillet even more enjoyable.

Must-Haves

Wooden Spoons: Metal utensils can scrape and ding the seasoning, leaving your cast iron vulnerable to rust and burnt spots. Wooden spoons are gentle.

Rubber-Tipped Tongs: Similarly, a good pair of tongs is essential, but you want to protect your skillet from scraping. Rubber-tipped tongs give you the best of both worlds.

Flexible Spatulas: Here's an exception: I prefer a metal spatula. It is flexible and has some spring in the movement, which is important when you're flipping eggs, grilled cheese, pancakes, etc. But use it so carefully—no scraping!

Chef's Knife: Every kitchen needs a good chef's knife, an all-purpose knife that can just as easily mince garlic as it can slice cheese.

Cutting Boards: In our home we have two cutting boards: a wood block that lives next to our stove and serves as a cutting station for pretty much everything, and a small plastic cutting board for meat. Because wood is porous, we don't cut meat on our wooden cutting board.

Nice-to-Haves

Lid: For a long time, before I bought a cast-iron Dutch oven with a lid that also fit my 12" skillet, I simply grabbed whatever lid I could find when I needed one. Occasionally I would even stick a baking sheet on top of the skillet, just to trap the heat in. A lid is by no means necessary, but you can purchase both cast-iron and glass lids made to fit your skillet.

Rubber Handle: These days, many new skillets come with a silicone sleeve that fits on the handle to protect your hand. These sleeves are certainly nice, but not a must-have.

Cast-Iron Brush: For ease of cleaning, I prefer a bristle brush that is specifically made for cast iron. These brushes make scouring much easier.

Chainmail Cleaner: Similarly, a specialty chainmail scouring pad can be a lovely addition to your cast-iron care kit.

Wire Pad: For the occasions when you need to deep clean and reseason your pan, a wire pad can be indispensable.

How to Use This Book

The recipes in this book were specifically developed with the 12" cast-iron skillet in mind, so although some of the recipes can be easily scaled up or down for other vessels, the 12" skillet is the ideal companion for this book.

As you enter the world of cast iron, I hope that you'll find these recipes easy and delicious—and also full of techniques that you can incorporate into your own recipes. The more you cook with your pan, the more comfortable you'll be with it, and I wholeheartedly believe that these recipes will launch you into a long and happy relationship with cast iron.

This book highlights recipes that are in constant rotation in my home. With full-time jobs and a young kid, our weekday cooking emphasizes what is fast, healthy, delicious, and can be made with a three-year-old "helper" standing on a stool in the kitchen asking for cheese every two minutes. We eat a mixture of vegetarian and meaty meals and try to pull from cuisines around the world. And if it can be made in one skillet, it's a favorite for everyone.

When I was teaching myself how to cook and bake, I loved the Julie & Julia–style approach of picking a book and cooking all the way through it. This method helped me become more comfortable baking bread, learning different techniques and flavor profiles, and gaining comfort and ease in the kitchen. My hope with this book is that after you've cooked your way through it, you'll have unleashed the full power of your cast-iron skillet. Happy cooking!

Cherry Tomato and Basil Quiche

CHAPTER 2: Breakfast and Brunch

Skillet Eggs and Bacon
Spinach and Mushroom Frittata
Chorizo and Cheddar Potato Hash
Tortilla Española
Cherry Tomato and Basil Quiche
Egg-in-a-Hole Breakfast Sandwich
French Toast with Berry Compote and Fresh Whipped Cream
Cheesy Migas
Fried Grits with Strawberries and Honey
Mediterranean Skillet Hash
Grits Breakfast Bake
Peanut Butter and Banana Baked Oatmeal
Smoked Salmon and Goat Cheese Frittata
Vegan Breakfast Skillet
Chilaquiles Rojos
Cottage Cheese and Banana Pancakes
Blackberry and White Chocolate Dutch Baby
Cheddar-Chive Biscuits and Spicy Sausage Gravy
Upside-Down Apple Cake
Sour Cream Coffee Cake

Skillet Eggs and Bacon

QUICK AND EASY → ONE-SKILLET MEAL

A skillet-fried egg with bacon drippings and a little butter is as close as you can come to perfection. My father was of the staunch opinion that this was the only way to fry an egg, and I'm not one to disagree with him (on this point). Frying eggs and bacon was his love language, something I could look forward to every time we saw him.

SERVES 4
PREP TIME: 5 MINUTES
COOK TIME: 20 TO 25 MINUTES

8 ounces thick-cut bacon

1 tablespoon salted butter

4 eggs

Pinch sea salt

1. Arrange the bacon in your skillet so that the pieces do not touch. He pan over medium-low heat and cook the bacon until it has begun to around the edges, about 10 minutes.

2. Flip the bacon and increase the heat to medium-high. Cook the baco 3 to 4 more minutes, until brown and crisp. Depending on your prefe you may want to flip the bacon once more to crisp it further.

3. Allow the pan to cool slightly and drain off the grease, leaving a resid layer.

4. Put the pan over medium heat and melt the butter. Crack the eggs in your skillet so that they are evenly spaced.

5. Sprinkle the yolks with salt.

6. Watch the egg carefully, using your spatula to gently free the edges egg white.

7. For an egg over easy: When the white has cooked through, after abo minutes, flip the egg while the yolk is still liquid. Cook for 1 minute an serve.

8. For an egg over medium: When the rim of the yolk has cooked throu after about 5 minutes, flip the egg and cook for 1 minute before servi

9. For an egg over well: When the yolk has almost completely cooked through, after about 6 minutes, flip the egg and cook for 1 more minu and serve.

Clean-up tip: Drain your grease into a glass or ceramic container. Once the grease has cooled, you can scrape it into the trash can to dispose.

Spinach and Mushroom Frittata

VEGETARIAN → ONE-SKILLET MEAL

Making a frittata is an easy way to feel very fancy, which is precisely what I'm looking for in a brunch food. This dish comes together quickly and with minimal effort.

SERVES 6

PREP TIME: 10 MINUTES

COOK TIME: 30 TO 40 MINUTES

2 tablespoons salted butter

1 white onion, chopped

2 garlic cloves, minced

2 cups cremini mushrooms, cleaned and sliced

2 cups fresh spinach

6 eggs

1 cup shredded mozzarella cheese

¼ cup heavy cream

Pinch sea salt

1. Preheat the oven to 400°F.

2. In your skillet, melt the butter over medium heat. Add the onion and and cook for 5 to 7 minutes, stirring occasionally until the onion begi soften.

3. Add the mushrooms and cook for an additional 5 minutes, until the mushrooms have browned.

4. Add the spinach to the pan, tossing a few times with the mushrooms onions.

5. While the spinach is wilting, whisk together the eggs, cheese, cream sea salt in a large bowl.

6. Spread the vegetable mix evenly across the skillet bottom and pour t egg mixture over the vegetables. Cook for 1 to 2 minutes or until the begin to set.

7. Transfer the skillet to the oven. Bake for 20 to 25 minutes, until the e have set.

Menu-planning tip: You can make the egg mixture in advance and store it in the refrigerator so that it's ready to go whenever you are.

Chorizo and Cheddar Potato Hash

ONE-SKILLET MEAL

Potato hash is one of my favorite breakfast-for-dinner (or "brinner") foods. It is filling and incredibly comforting to eat, plus the cast-iron skillet cooks up the potatoes perfectly crispy on all the edges. I love this topped with a fried egg or two—the runnier the yolk, the better.

SERVES 4

PREP TIME: 15 MINUTES

COOK TIME: 25 TO 30 MINUTES

8 ounces chorizo sausage, coarsely chopped

2 tablespoons salted butter

1 white onion, chopped

2 garlic cloves, minced

2 cups shredded potatoes (1 to 2 Yukon Gold)

½ teaspoon sea salt

¼ pound cheddar cheese, grated

1. Warm your skillet over medium heat. Once it is hot, add the chorizo. for 8 to 10 minutes, stirring frequently, until browned and crisp. Remo the chorizo from the pan and set aside.

2. Add the butter, onion, and garlic to the pan. Cook for 3 to 4 minutes, the onions have begun to soften. Stir in the potatoes and salt and mi thoroughly. Spread evenly so the potatoes are distributed in a layer a the bottom of the pan. Cook for 7 to 10 minutes, until the potatoes ha browned and crisped.

3. Use a spatula to flip the potatoes. Cook for an additional 5 to 7 minut until they are browned on both sides.

4. Remove the pan from the heat and stir in the cheese and chorizo. Se hot.

Substitution tip: If chorizo is difficult for you to get your hands on, try using spicy Italian sausage.

Tortilla Española

VEGETARIAN → ONE-SKILLET MEAL

One of my favorite things about being in my thirties (and bless, there are so many) is that hanging out with friends looks very different than it did 10 years ago. There's way fewer late nights and way more dinner parties where everyone contributes something, and we all eat until we're stuffed and enjoy the pure pleasure of each other's company. The first time I had a tortilla Española—a potato omelet that is a signature dish in Spanish cuisine—was at one such weekend with friends, and I think I must have eaten three portions slathered with aioli and served with a handful of fresh cherry tomatoes. It was heaven!

SERVES 6 TO 8

PREP TIME: 15 MINUTES

COOK TIME: 35 TO 40 MINUTES

2 cups olive oil

2 Yukon Gold potatoes, peeled and thinly sliced

1 large white onion

8 large eggs

Pinch sea salt

1. Heat the oil in your skillet over medium-low heat.

2. Add the potatoes and onions to the skillet and simmer until tender, 2 minutes.

3. Strain the potatoes and onions into a bowl and drain off the oil, settin aside 2 tablespoons.

4. Whisk the eggs in a large bowl until frothing. Stir the potatoes and on into the eggs, along with the salt.

5. Return 1 tablespoon of olive oil to the pan and heat over medium he When the oil is hot, pour the egg and potato mixture into the pan, co for 7 to 10 minutes. When the eggs have set and the bottom has star brown, remove the pan from the heat.

6. Place a plate—large enough to cover the entire skillet—on top and fl tortilla out of the pan. Return the pan to the heat, adding the remaini olive oil, and slide the tortilla back into the pan, golden-side up. Cook an additional 5 minutes, until both sides are golden brown. Flip once onto a plate, slice, and serve.

> Menu-planning tip: Make a quick and easy "aioli" dip for your tortilla by whisking ½ cup of mayonnaise, the juice of 1 lemon, 1 garlic clove (minced), 1 teaspoon of paprika, and a pinch of salt.

Cherry Tomato and Basil Quiche

VEGETARIAN → ONE-SKILLET MEAL

A few years ago I made a big change in my approach to making quiche, switching from a classic flaky pastry crust to a pizza dough crust. Pizza dough is slightly heartier than pastry dough, but it crisps up wonderfully in the cast-iron skillet, ensuring that there is nary a soggy bottom in sight.

SERVES 6
PREP TIME: 25 MINUTES
INACTIVE TIME: 1 HOUR
COOK TIME: 40 MINUTES

FOR THE CRUST

2 tablespoons olive oil, plus more for greasing

¼ cup warm water

1 tablespoon active dry yeast

Pinch sea salt

Pinch red pepper flakes

2 cups bread flour, plus more for kneading

FOR THE FILLING

1 teaspoon olive oil, plus more for greasing

8 eggs

¼ cup whole milk

2 cups cherry tomatoes, halved

1 cup fresh basil, coarsely chopped, plus 2 tablespoons for topping

1 small red onion, chopped

2 garlic cloves, minced

Pinch sea salt

½ cup crumbled goat cheese

1. Coat a large bowl with olive oil and set aside.
2. In another large bowl, mix 2 tablespoons of olive oil, water, yeast, sa red pepper flakes. Let the mixture sit for 1 minute.
3. With a wooden spoon, stir the flour into the olive oil mixture, ½ cup a time, until it forms a loose ball.
4. Turn the dough out onto a floured surface and knead for 5 to 7 minut until stretchy and pliable.
5. Transfer the dough to the oiled bowl, turn once, and cover lightly with towel. Allow the dough to rise in a warm place for 1 hour.
6. Preheat the oven to 350°F.
7. Grease your skillet with olive oil.
8. In a large bowl, whisk together the eggs and milk.
9. Stir in the tomatoes, basil, onion, garlic, and salt.
10. Press the dough into the skillet across the bottom and up the sides. the filling into the crust.
11. Brush the edges of the crust with 1 teaspoon of olive oil.
12. Bake for 40 minutes, or until the eggs are cooked through and the cr golden brown.
13. Top with fresh basil and serve warm.

> Substitution tip: If you're looking for a flaky and buttery alternative, try this quiche with a traditional short crust pie dough (see here).

Egg-in-a-Hole Breakfast Sandwich

QUICK AND EASY → ONE-SKILLET MEAL

My husband, Dan, and I started dating in college, and part of our early courtship involved flexing our culinary muscles to impress each other in my small off-campus apartment kitchen. Back in the olden days of the internet, there were only a handful of food blogs, so we mostly cooked things we could find on Food Network's website and, occasionally, things we were confident making from our own childhoods. Dan gleefully brought "toad in a hole" into our relationship, a breakfast delicacy that I had not grown up with but have come to love. It's simple, it's fast, and the cast-iron skillet's nonstick surface makes flipping a breeze. Bonus: It makes a next-level delicious breakfast sandwich with the simple addition of bacon and cheese.

SERVES 1

PREP TIME: 5 MINUTES

COOK TIME: 15 TO 20 MINUTES

2 slices bacon

2 thick-cut slices bread

1 tablespoon salted butter

2 large eggs

Pinch sea salt

¼ cup shredded cheddar cheese

1. Arrange the bacon in your pan so that the pieces do not touch. Heat pan over medium-low heat and cook the bacon until it has begun to around the edges, about 10 minutes.

2. Flip the bacon and increase the heat to medium-high. Cook for anoth to 4 minutes, until brown and crisp. Depending on your preference, y

may want to flip the bacon once more to crisp it further.

3. Set the bacon aside and drain the grease from the pan.

4. Use a cookie cutter to cut a 2" hole in the center of each slice of brea you don't have a circle-shaped cutter, a small glass jar works well, to

5. Heat the skillet over medium-high heat. When the pan is hot, add the butter. Put the slices of bread in the skillet and reduce the heat to me

6. Crack an egg into each of the holes, sprinkle with sea salt, and cook minutes.

7. Flip the egg and the bread together. For an egg over easy, cook for 1 minute. For an egg over medium, cook for 2 more minutes, and for a over well, cook for 3 more minutes.

8. Build a sandwich with the bacon and cheese between the two slices bread.

Substitution tip: Swap fried bologna for the bacon for a truly delightful twist.

French Toast with Berry Compote and Fresh Whipped Cream

VEGETARIAN

French toast is one of my son's favorite foods to order when we go out for brunch. And really, what's not to love? The decadent restaurant portions are usually bigger than his face and frequently served with fruit and whipped cream. At home the portions are slightly smaller, but he's always impressed when I tell him I whipped up a fresh berry compote and I let him dollop out his own whipped cream, making this the all-around dream meal, hands down. (Just kidding—my three-year-old doesn't know what compote is; he just loves berries.)

SERVES 4

PREP TIME: 15 MINUTES

COOK TIME: 40 MINUTES

FOR THE COMPOTE

1 cup fresh strawberries, diced

1 cup fresh blueberries

1 cup fresh blackberries

2 tablespoons honey

Zest of 1 lemon

Pinch sea salt

FOR THE FRENCH TOAST

4 eggs

½ cup whole milk

1 tablespoon sugar

1 teaspoon vanilla extract

1 teaspoon ground cinnamon

1 teaspoon ground ginger

4 tablespoons salted butter, divided

1 loaf crusty bread, cut into ¾ to 1" slices

FOR THE WHIPPED CREAM

1 cup heavy whipping cream

2 tablespoons sugar

1 teaspoon vanilla extract

1. In a medium saucepan, combine the strawberries, blueberries, blackberries, honey, lemon zest, and salt.

2. Bring to a gentle boil, stirring occasionally. Reduce the heat to low an simmer, stirring frequently, for 5 more minutes.

3. Set aside to cool.

4. In a large shallow bowl, whisk together the eggs, milk, sugar, vanilla, cinnamon, and ginger.

5. Preheat your skillet over medium-high heat. Add 1 tablespoon of but melt.

6. Dip a slice of bread into the egg mixture, submerging it completely a turning it for a full coating. Place it in the hot skillet.

7. Cook the bread for 2 to 3 minutes per side until crisp and browned. K the French toast warm in the microwave, covered loosely with a kitch towel.

8. Repeat with each slice of bread.

9. While the bread is cooking, combine the cream, sugar, and vanilla. W stand or handheld mixer, whip the cream until it forms stiff peaks. Se aside.

10. Serve warm, topped with a generous drizzle of berry compote and a of whipped cream.

Ingredient tip: For a late-summer twist, try fresh peaches instead of berries in your compote.

Cheesy Migas

VEGETARIAN → QUICK AND EASY → ONE-SKILLET MEAL

The word migas means different things in different places. In Spain or Portugal it likely includes day-old bread and other ingredients such as spinach and pork ribs and is served either as a breakfast dish or as a side to a main dish. In Mexico, migas means leftover tortillas with eggs—unless you're in Mexico City, where it is garlic soup with leftover bread and a raw egg cooked in the soup. And finally, inspiring this recipe, is the Tex-Mex migas: It takes the hearty version from Mexico and adds onions, cheese, and other condiments. No matter how you define it, migas is a delicious meal that makes use of leftovers to create something brand new.

SERVES 4
PREP TIME: 5 MINUTES
COOK TIME: 15 TO 20 MINUTES

2 tablespoons olive oil

2 tablespoons salted butter

5 or 6 corn tortillas, cut into ½" strips

1 jalapeño pepper, seeded and minced

1 small white onion, minced

2 garlic cloves, minced

6 eggs

¼ cup heavy cream

Pinch red pepper flakes

Pinch sea salt

¼ cup shredded cheddar cheese

¼ cup shredded pepper Jack cheese

½ cup chopped cilantro

1. Combine the olive oil and butter in your skillet over medium-high hea the tortillas and cook for about 5 minutes, stirring frequently until bro and crisped.

2. Turn down the heat to medium and add the jalapeño, onion, and garl the pan, and sauté for 3 to 4 minutes.

3. In a medium bowl, whisk together the eggs, cream, red pepper flake salt. Pour the egg mixture into the pan and cook for 5 to 6 minutes, s frequently.

4. Stir in the cheese, and cook for an additional 1 to 2 minutes, until the cheese has melted.

5. Serve hot, topped with the cilantro.

Menu-planning tip: Serve in a large bowl alongside Spicy Black Beans with Cotija.

Fried Grits with Strawberries and Honey

VEGETARIAN

Grits, for anyone who is not familiar with them, are the coarser version of dried corn that has been ground in a stone mill. The finer product is cornmeal. Although both are beautiful things, grits are life. I love grits in all forms: cheesy and salty on the side of my breakfast, creamy and served topped with a generous portion of shrimp and sauce, and fried up into cakes and served with fresh fruit and a drizzle of honey for breakfast.

SERVES 4 TO 6

PREP TIME: 20 MINUTES

INACTIVE TIME: 1 HOUR (OR OVERNIGHT)

COOK TIME: 40 MINUTES

½ cup stone-ground grits

1 cup water

1 cup whole milk

1 tablespoon honey

Pinch sea salt

1 teaspoon ground cinnamon

4 tablespoons salted butter

½ cup all-purpose flour

FOR THE TOPPING

1 pint fresh strawberries, hulled and sliced

3 tablespoons honey

2 tablespoons powdered sugar

1. In a medium saucepan combine the grits, water, milk, honey, salt, an cinnamon. Bring to a boil and then reduce the heat to a simmer. Coo about 20 minutes, stirring frequently, until the grits are thick but still creamy.

2. Using a small amount of the butter, grease a 9 x 9" baking dish and the grit mixture into the pan. Chill for at least 1 hour, preferably overn

3. Combine the strawberries and honey for the topping and set aside.

4. Melt 1 tablespoon of butter in your skillet over medium heat.

5. Slice the grits into 3" squares. Use a spoon to coat the top and botto the squares with flour.

6. Transfer 4 squares to the hot skillet and fry for 2 to 3 minutes per sid crispy.

7. As the grits squares come off the skillet, keep them warm in the micr or in a 200°F oven on a baking sheet.

8. Fry the remaining squares, adding butter to the pan between each b

9. Serve hot, topped with the fresh berries and honey and a sprinkle of powdered sugar.

Fun tip: Instead of using a baking pan, pour the grits into a greased cupcake pan for rounds!

Mediterranean Skillet Hash

VEGETARIAN → QUICK AND EASY → ONE-SKILLET MEAL

When we were trying to get pregnant with our second child, I read that a Mediterranean diet was good for fertility. As anyone who has ever tried to get pregnant can attest, you'll do basically anything to make things happen. I was wide open to whatever combination of science, witchcraft, and old wives' tales would result in a healthy baby, which mostly meant that for a few months I ate a lot of olives. We tried lots of different recipes with a "Mediterranean" twist, and some of them were delicious enough that they stuck around to become family favorites.

SERVES 4
PREP TIME: 15 MINUTES
COOK TIME: 15 MINUTES

2 tablespoons olive oil

6 small red potatoes, diced

3 garlic cloves, minced

1 red bell pepper, diced

Pinch sea salt

1 small red onion, minced

½ cup kalamata olives, halved

½ cup feta crumbles

¼ cup roasted red peppers, drained and chopped

¼ cup fresh flat-leaf parsley, chopped

1. Heat the oil in your skillet over medium heat. Add the potatoes and c for 2 to 3 minutes, stirring frequently.

2. Add the garlic, bell pepper, and salt. Continue to cook for 10 to 12 mi stirring frequently, until the potatoes are browned and cooked throug

3. Remove from the heat and top with the onion, olives, feta, roasted re peppers, and parsley. Serve hot.

Ingredient tip: Add a sweet potato, cubed, for a boost of iron and calcium.

Grits Breakfast Bake

Have I mentioned how much I love grits? A casserole really plays to the strength of grits, which I firmly believe are versatile enough to shine both when they're creamy and when they're asked to take a more solid state. When mixed with sausage and cheddar, this grits bake embodies everything a breakfast casserole should be—firm but creamy, crispy around the edges, salty and cheesy, and comforting.

SERVES 4 TO 6

PREP TIME: 10 MINUTES

COOK TIME: 1 HOUR

1 cup stone-ground grits

3 cups water

1 cup whole milk

½ teaspoon sea salt

8 ounces ground sausage

1 white onion, chopped

2 garlic cloves, minced

2 tablespoons butter, divided

3 large eggs

1 cup cheddar cheese, shredded

¼ teaspoon red pepper flakes

1. Heat the oven to 350°F.

2. In a medium saucepan, combine the grits, water, milk, and salt over heat. Bring to a boil and then reduce the heat to low. Simmer the grit stirring frequently, until they are thick but still creamy, about 20 minut

3. While the grits are cooking, heat your skillet over medium-high heat.

4. Add the sausage, onion, garlic, and 1 tablespoon of butter to the skill Cook for 5 to 7 minutes, stirring frequently, until the sausage has coo through.

5. In a large bowl, whisk the eggs, then stir in the grits, along with the cheese, remaining butter, and red pepper flakes.

6. Pour the grits mixture into the skillet, stirring well to incorporate the sausage and onion.

7. Transfer the skillet to the oven and bake for 35 to 45 minutes, until s Serve hot.

Substitution tip: For a vegetarian twist, swap out the sausage and cheddar for spinach and feta.

Peanut Butter and Banana Baked Oatmeal

VEGETARIAN → ONE-SKILLET MEAL

This baked oatmeal is a favorite in my house because it includes all the things my hungry three-year-old loves (namely bananas and peanut butter) and is filling enough that he doesn't mention food to me for at least a few hours after breakfast. To streamline weekday breakfast, I like to make one batch of oatmeal for the week and parse out portions each morning.

SERVES 4
PREP TIME: 5 MINUTES
COOK TIME: 40 TO 45 MINUTES

2 cups rolled oats

2 ripe bananas, sliced

1 tablespoon packed brown sugar

1 teaspoon baking powder

½ teaspoon sea salt

2 eggs

1½ cups whole milk

¼ cup honey

3 tablespoons salted butter, room temperature

½ cup smooth peanut butter

1. Preheat the oven to 350°F.

2. In a large bowl, stir together the oats, bananas, brown sugar, baking powder, and salt.

3. In a medium bowl, whisk together the eggs, milk, honey, and butter.

4. Fold the milk mixture into the oat mixture. Spoon half of the batter int skillet.

5. Swirl half of the peanut butter into the batter, then top with the remai half.

6. Bake for 40 to 45 minutes or until crisp around the edges and cooke through. Serve hot.

Toddler tips: If you're taking the frazzled parent approach to this dish, allow the oatmeal to cool to room temperature before portioning it into containers to refrigerate. Any trapped steam will make the oatmeal gluey. For children under one year old, substitute maple syrup or agave for honey.

Smoked Salmon and Goat Cheese Frittata

QUICK AND EASY → ONE-SKILLET MEAL

Smoked salmon is one of my favorite foods. For me, at least, it was the gateway salmon. I fell in love with the pure heaven of an everything bagel loaded with cream cheese, lox, red onions, and capers, and before I knew it, I was making my own dill sauce for broiled salmon. This frittata gives the salmon a platform to really shine, pairing it with two stalwart companions: creamy goat cheese and fresh dill.

SERVES 6
PREP TIME: 10 MINUTES
COOK TIME: 15 TO 20 MINUTES

2 tablespoons salted butter

1 white onion, chopped

2 garlic cloves, minced

6 eggs

1 cup crumbled goat cheese

¼ cup heavy cream

Pinch sea salt

8 ounces smoked salmon, coarsely chopped

3 tablespoons minced fresh dill

1. Preheat the oven to 400°F.

2. In your skillet, melt the butter over medium heat. Add the onions and and cook for 3 to 5 minutes, stirring occasionally until the onions hav begun to soften.

3. In a large bowl, whisk together the eggs, cheese, cream, and salt.

4. Stir the smoked salmon into the egg mixture and pour it into the skill the onions. Cook for 1 to 2 minutes or until the eggs begin to set. Tra the skillet to the oven.

5. Bake for 8 to 10 minutes, until the eggs have set.

6. Top with the fresh dill and serve warm.

> Menu-planning tip: If you want to take this an extra fancy step further, whip up a simple dill sauce to go with it. Combine 1 cup of Greek yogurt, the juice of 1 lemon, and a handful of chopped fresh dill.

Vegan Breakfast Skillet

VEGAN → QUICK AND EASY → ONE-SKILLET MEAL

This rich and hearty breakfast skillet is loaded with delicious vegetables for a combination that is filling and packed full of flavor.

SERVES 4
PREP TIME: 15 MINUTES
COOK TIME: 15 MINUTES

2 tablespoons olive oil

1 sweet potato, peeled and chopped

3 red potatoes, chopped

1 white onion, diced

3 garlic cloves, minced

1 red bell pepper, diced

¼ teaspoon sea salt, plus a pinch

1 small red onion, finely chopped

1 avocado, peeled, pitted, and sliced

¼ cup fresh cilantro, chopped

Squeeze of fresh lime

1. Heat the oil in your skillet over medium heat. Add the sweet potato, r potatoes, and onion, and cook for 2 to 3 minutes, stirring frequently.

2. Add the garlic, bell pepper, and salt. Continue to cook for 10 to 12 mi stirring frequently, until the potatoes are browned and cooked throug

3. Top with the red onion, avocado, cilantro, lime juice, and a pinch of s

> Ingredient tip: Get more protein into this dish by adding black beans or tofu.

Chilaquiles Rojos

VEGETARIAN → QUICK AND EASY → ONE-SKILLET MEAL

Like their cousin, migas, chilaquiles give new life to leftover corn tortillas. Hailing from Mexico, chilaquiles come with a rojo or verde sauce and can be served with a fried egg, beans, cotija cheese, and avocado for a full brunch meal.

SERVES 4
PREP TIME: 20 MINUTES
COOK TIME: 10 MINUTES

¼ cup vegetable oil, plus 1 tablespoon

12 corn tortillas, cut into quarters

Pinch sea salt

2 large tomatoes, diced

1 small white onion, diced

1 jalapeño pepper, seeded and sliced

3 garlic cloves, minced

1½ cups vegetable broth, divided

1 tablespoon tomato paste

1 teaspoon dried oregano

¼ teaspoon ground cumin

½ teaspoon red pepper flakes

1 avocado, peeled, pitted, and sliced

½ cup fresh cilantro, chopped

¼ cup cotija cheese

2 radishes, thinly sliced

1. Heat ¼ cup of oil in your skillet over medium-high heat. Once the oil shimmering, fry the tortilla pieces (working in batches, if necessary) f 3 minutes, then flip. Fry an additional 1 to 2 minutes until golden bro

2. Transfer the chips to a rack to cool and sprinkle with salt.

3. Remove the pan from the heat and drain the oil.

4. In a food processor, blend the tomatoes, onion, jalapeño, and garlic.

5. Heat the remaining tablespoon of oil in the skillet over medium heat. the pan is warm, add the salsa mixture to the skillet, along with half o broth and all of the tomato paste. Stir in the oregano, cumin, red pep flakes, and a pinch of salt.

6. Cook, stirring frequently, until the sauce has thickened to coat the ba a spoon. As necessary, add more broth.

7. Add the tortilla chips and stir to coat. Cook for 3 to 5 minutes until the tortilla chips are warm and well coated.

8. Serve warm with the avocado, cilantro, cotija, and radishes.

Menu-planning tip: Try adding a fried or scrambled egg to make this a heartier meal.

Cottage Cheese and Banana Pancakes

VEGETARIAN → QUICK AND EASY → ONE-SKILLET MEAL

When I was first introducing my son to solid foods, I had a field day trying different flavors and textures. I aimed to make finger foods that he could pick up on his own in order to strengthen his pincer grasp, and I delighted in watching him eat. He remains a voracious eater and was a most enthusiastic recipe tester for this cookbook. During those early days, these pancakes were in regular rotation because they're quick and easy. More experienced eaters will delight in the way cottage cheese elevates the simple pancake with tang, texture, and extra moistness.

SERVES 2 TO 4

PREP TIME: 10 MINUTES

COOK TIME: 10 MINUTES

1 banana, mashed

½ cup cottage cheese

½ cup rolled oats

2 eggs

1 teaspoon vanilla extract

2 tablespoons salted butter

Honey, for serving

Fresh fruit, for serving

1. In a medium bowl, whisk together the banana, cottage cheese, oats, and vanilla.

2. Melt the butter in your skillet over medium heat. Use a large spoon to dollop 4 silver dollar–size pancakes into the skillet, keeping them tow the center of the pan.

3. Cook for 3 to 4 minutes, until the pancakes have started to brown an bubble. Flip and cook an additional 1 to 2 minutes. Remove and repe with the remaining batter.

4. Serve warm with a drizzle of honey or fresh fruit.

Ingredient tip: For an even simpler pancake recipe that's perfect for babies, combine 1 banana, 1 egg, and ½ cup of oats and follow the same cooking instructions.

Blackberry and White Chocolate Dutch Baby

VEGETARIAN

There is something magical about the way a Dutch baby (German pancake) comes together. I love the way they puff up and how they are light yet buttery. Pancakes are not my particular strength (and therefore fall squarely on the shoulders of my husband in our division of domestic duties), but for some reason I can pull off a perfect Dutch baby, which feels way more impressive.

SERVES 2 TO 4

PREP TIME: 20 MINUTES

COOK TIME: 20 MINUTES

1 cup buttermilk

3 eggs

2 tablespoons packed brown sugar

1 teaspoon vanilla extract

Pinch sea salt

¾ cup all-purpose flour

5 tablespoons salted butter

1 cup fresh blackberries

2 tablespoons honey

½ cup white chocolate chips

Maple syrup, for serving

1. Adjust your oven rack to the middle position, place your empty skillet and preheat the oven to 425°F.

2. In a medium bowl, whisk together the buttermilk, eggs, brown sugar, vanilla, and salt.

3. Fold in the flour gently until blended. Let the batter rest for 5 minutes

4. Remove the hot skillet from the oven, add the butter, and let it melt.

5. Pour the batter into the skillet and immediately return it to the oven. for 15 to 20 minutes or until the pancake is golden brown and the sid have risen. Then remove it from the oven.

6. While the pancake bakes, toss the blackberries and honey in a small

7. In a microwave-safe bowl, melt the white chocolate in the microwave 20 seconds, stirring, and repeating 1 or 2 more times until smooth.

8. Cut the hot pancake into wedges. Top the slices with blackberries an drizzle of white chocolate. Serve with maple syrup or honey for dippi

Ingredient tip: A Dutch baby is a lovely base for all sorts of fresh fruits, depending on the season. Strawberries and honey, blueberries and lemon curd, or peaches and fresh cream are all delightful combinations.

Cheddar-Chive Biscuits and Spicy Sausage Gravy

ONE-SKILLET MEAL

Biscuits and gravy always makes me think of a breakfast buffet, with a warming pan full of hot sausage gravy and a steaming pile of biscuits. It tastes like nostalgia, like breakfasts out with my grandma at Southern cafeterias—a happy memory full of food that feels like a hug. This recipe achieves a similar effect, minus the buffet table.

SERVES 4
PREP TIME: 20 MINUTES
COOK TIME: 30 MINUTES

FOR THE BISCUITS

1 cup all-purpose flour, plus more for kneading

½ teaspoon baking soda

½ teaspoon baking powder

½ teaspoon sea salt

½ cup shredded cheddar cheese

¼ cup minced fresh chives

4 tablespoons cold, salted butter, plus more for greasing

½ cup buttermilk

FOR THE GRAVY

6 ounces ground hot pork sausage

2 garlic cloves, minced

2 tablespoons all-purpose flour

1 cup whole milk

Sea salt, for seasoning

½ teaspoon freshly ground black pepper

¼ teaspoon red pepper flakes

1. Heat the oven to 425°F.

2. In a medium bowl, mix the flour, baking soda, baking powder, salt, ch cheese, and chives.

3. Cut the butter into cubes and add it to the flour mixture. Mix together your hands, crumbling until the texture resembles coarse cornmeal.

4. Stir in the buttermilk.

5. On a floured work surface, pat the dough out into a large rectangle. the dough in half and turn and pat it out again into a large rectangle. Repeat this process 3 to 4 times, folding the dough in half and rotatin Add flour as you work to keep the dough from sticking.

6. Pat the dough out to 1½ to 2" thickness. Use a biscuit cutter to cut th biscuits into rounds. (If you don't have this tool, a jar lid works well.)

7. Grease your skillet with butter. Arrange the dough rounds in the skille toward the center so they are nice and snug. (This helps with rise!)

8. Bake for 15 to 20 minutes or until cooked through and golden brown.

9. Transfer the biscuits to a cooling rack and quickly wipe out the skillet cloth dishrag.

10. Add the sausage and garlic to the skillet, and cook for 3 to 5 minutes medium-high heat until the sausage is browned.

11. Stir in the flour, and continue cooking until it is fully incorporated.

12. Pour in the milk, whisking quickly until the gravy thickens and bubble

13. Season with salt, pepper, and red pepper flakes.

14. Top each biscuit with a generous portion of gravy and serve warm.

> Substitution tip: For a vegetarian option, substitute 2 cups of coarsely chopped mushrooms for sausage.

Upside-Down Apple Cake

VEGETARIAN

An upside-down cake is a visual showstopper, with the fruit happily nestled into the cake, crisp and browned and light and fluffy all at the same time. Apples are particularly well suited to this style of cake, as they hold their shape and caramelize so beautifully. It's a stunning brunch centerpiece that's so satisfying to eat.

SERVES 6
PREP TIME: 15 MINUTES
COOK TIME: 45 MINUTES

FOR THE APPLES

½ cup brown sugar

1 stick salted butter

4 or 5 Granny Smith apples, peeled, cored, and cut into slices

FOR THE CAKE

1 stick salted butter, room temperature

¾ cup granulated sugar

2 eggs

1 teaspoon vanilla extract

1½ cups all-purpose flour

½ teaspoon baking soda

1 teaspoon baking powder

½ teaspoon sea salt

¾ cup Greek yogurt

Honey for drizzling

1. Preheat the oven to 375°F.

2. In your skillet, combine the brown sugar and butter over medium hea well and then place the apples into the skillet, making sure the slices lying flat on their sides.

3. Lower the heat to a simmer and allow the mixture to caramelize.

4. In a large bowl, using a handheld mixer or a stand mixer, cream the and sugar.

5. Add in the eggs, one at a time, mixing in each egg completely before adding the next.

6. Add in the vanilla.

7. In a separate bowl, mix together the flour, baking soda, baking powd and salt. Add the dry mixture to the wet batter ⅓ at a time, alternatin adding the Greek yogurt ¼ cup at a time.

8. Mix well, making sure to scrape the bottom of the bowl to catch any pockets of flour.

9. Remove the skillet from the heat when the apples start to brown and soften. Spoon the batter over the apples.

10. Bake for 20 to 25 minutes, until the cake is cooked through and gold brown.

11. Allow to cool in the skillet for 5 minutes before turning the cake out o your serving dish.

12. Top with a drizzle of honey and serve.

Ingredient tip: For a spring twist, stir halved fresh strawberries into this cake batter recipe and follow the baking instructions.

Sour Cream Coffee Cake

VEGETARIAN

Coffee cake is a classic for a reason: moist cake topped with a spiced crumb and filled with a buttery swirl. It's lovely with a cup of coffee (duh) or tea, and it's both elegant enough to be served on Christmas morning (my family's tradition) and easy enough to adorn a weekend brunch table. The addition of sour cream in this cake adds moistness and also a tang, which plays nicely off the strong spice of the cinnamon, ginger, and cloves.

SERVES 6 TO 8

PREP TIME: 20 MINUTES

COOK TIME: 40 TO 45 MINUTES

FOR THE FILLING

1½ cups packed brown sugar

1 cup chopped walnuts

½ cup all-purpose flour

1 stick salted butter, room temperature

2 tablespoons ground cinnamon

1 tablespoon ground ginger

1 tablespoon ground cloves

FOR THE CAKE

3 cups all-purpose flour

2 teaspoons baking powder

1 teaspoon sea salt

2 sticks salted butter, room temperature

1 cup granulated sugar

1 teaspoon vanilla extract

3 eggs

1½ cups sour cream

1. In a medium bowl, stir together the brown sugar, walnuts, flour, butte cinnamon, ginger, and cloves. Set aside.

2. Preheat the oven to 350°F.

3. In a separate medium bowl, combine the flour, baking powder, and s

4. Using a hand mixer or a stand mixer, cream the butter and sugar tog until light and fluffy. Add in the vanilla and then the eggs, one at a tim mixing until each egg is fully incorporated.

5. Add ⅓ of the dry flour mixture to the batter, then alternate with ½ cup sour cream. Continue alternating until all the ingredients are fully incorporated.

6. Pour half of the batter into your skillet. Top with half of the filling. Lay remaining batter on top, followed by the remaining filling.

7. Bake for 40 to 45 minutes or until cooked through. Serve warm.

Leftovers tip: A day-old slice of coffee cake warmed in the toaster is just about perfection.

Classic Cinnamon Rolls

CHAPTER 3: Breads

Garlic Naan
Pizza Margherita
Classic Cinnamon Rolls
Iced Lemon Scones
Masa Harina Cornbread
English Muffins
Pull-Apart Garlic Knots
Rosemary and Garlic Focaccia
Buttermilk Biscuits
Pita Bread

Garlic Naan

VEGETARIAN

When I was growing up, Indian food was not a regular part of our family's menu. In high school, friends whose families had broader palates introduced me to cuisines from around the world, but it wasn't until college that I really got hooked on a few classic Indian takeout dishes. Like all good college stories, this one takes place at two in the morning and involves takeout from a dubiously named restaurant (in this case, Pizza Galerry, which is not a typo). The quality of its pizza was questionable, but the tikka masala and garlic naan were superb. I've since expanded my palate beyond tikka masala, but I still love garlic naan and clamor at any opportunity to make and eat it. In a cast-iron skillet, which can be hot and dry, the buttery bread puffs up and browns beautifully.

SERVES 6 TO 8

PREP TIME: 15 MINUTES

INACTIVE TIME: 2 HOURS 10 MINUTES

COOK TIME: 20 MINUTES

2 tablespoons dry active yeast

1 tablespoon sugar

¼ cup olive oil, plus more for greasing

¼ cup warm water

5 cups bread flour

2 teaspoons baking powder

1 cup full-fat plain yogurt

½ cup whole milk

1 stick salted butter, melted

5 garlic cloves, minced

¼ cup chopped cilantro

1 tablespoon sea salt

1. In a large bowl, combine the yeast, sugar, olive oil, and water. Stir w let it sit for 10 minutes.

2. In another bowl, mix the flour and baking powder.

3. Using a whisk, mix the yogurt and milk into the yeast mixture. Add th mixture, a little at a time, mixing first with a wooden spoon and then hands.

4. Knead with your hands for 2 to 3 minutes, until a soft, smooth dough forms.

5. Coat a glass bowl with olive oil. Place the dough ball in the bowl, turn once, and cover with a towel. Allow the dough to rise in a warm spot. dough should double in size after about 2 hours.

6. Turn the dough out onto a floured surface and punch it down slightly. Divide into 10 equal portions and roll each into an oblong shape. The dough should be ¼" thick.

7. In a small bowl, combine the melted butter and minced garlic. Brush dough round with the garlic butter.

8. Heat your skillet over medium-high heat.

9. Place a dough round on the hot skillet, butter-side down. Cook for 1 minutes, until the dough begins to brown. Brush the top side with gar butter and flip.

10. Cook for an additional 1 to 2 minutes until the bottom side is golden Repeat with the remaining dough.

11. As the naan comes off the skillet, brush it once more with garlic butte put it in an oven or microwave to keep it warm.

12. Sprinkle with cilantro and salt and serve warm.

> Meal-planning tip: Leftover naan can be toasted and used as bread to level up just about any sandwich in a truly spectacular fashion.

<u>Pizza Margherita</u>

VEGETARIAN → ONE-SKILLET MEAL

Pizza Margherita is one of life's true pleasures. Its beauty lies in its simplicity. There are just a few toppings, but when it's made with truly quality ingredients, it shines.

SERVES 4 TO 6

PREP TIME: 15 MINUTES

INACTIVE TIME: 1 HOUR 25 MINUTES

COOK TIME: 12 TO 15 MINUTES

FOR THE DOUGH

1½ tablespoons olive oil, plus more for greasing

1 tablespoon dry active yeast

1 tablespoon sea salt

¾ cup warm water

2½ cups bread flour, plus more for kneading

FOR THE SAUCE

1 cup pureed tomatoes

2 tablespoons tomato paste

3 garlic cloves, minced

1 teaspoon olive oil

1 teaspoon sea salt

FOR THE TOPPINGS

1 cup freshly grated mozzarella cheese

¼ cup fresh basil, coarsely chopped

Sea salt

Olive oil to drizzle

1. Whisk together the olive oil, yeast, salt, and water. Whisk until fully incorporated and frothing. Let sit for 10 minutes.

2. Add half the flour and stir with a wooden spoon. Add the remaining fl and use your hands to knead together. Knead for 10 minutes, until th dough ball is smooth and pliable.

3. Coat a glass bowl with olive oil. Place the dough ball in the bowl, turn once, and cover with a towel. Allow the dough to rise in a warm spot.

4. The dough should double in size after about 1 hour. Punch the doug down and allow it to rise for 15 more minutes.

5. While the dough is rising, combine the pureed tomatoes, tomato pas garlic, olive oil, and salt in a medium saucepan. Bring to a boil, whisk and then reduce the heat to a simmer. Allow to simmer, stirring occasionally, while the dough rises.

6. Heat the oven to 500°F. Place your skillet in the oven.

7. Turn the dough onto a floured work surface. Knead for 5 to 7 minute the dough is pliable and stretches nicely without tearing.

8. Roll the dough into a 14" round, flouring as you go to keep it from sti and tearing.

9. Remove the skillet from the oven and coat it with olive oil. Transfer th dough into the skillet, pressing it slightly up the edges.

10. Use a ladle to spread the sauce evenly across the dough. Evenly dis the mozzarella and half the basil. Sprinkle with salt and finish with a of olive oil.

11. Bake for 12 to 15 minutes, until the pizza crust is golden brown and t cheese has melted.

12. Top with the remaining basil and serve warm.

Substitution tip: This pizza dough recipe and method will work for many different toppings. So bust out the pineapple and Canadian bacon, or swap the marinara for pesto and add sausage—whatever sounds good!

Classic Cinnamon Rolls

VEGETARIAN

One of the greatest frustrations of having celiac disease is being able to smell the cinnamon buns cooking at the mall but never being able to eat said cinnamon buns. Instead I am forced to make my own (gluten-free) cinnamon buns, which has the one big silver lining of making my own house smell delightful. Plus, unlike the mall version, the ones you make at home taste as good as they smell.

SERVES 8

PREP TIME: 20 MINUTES

INACTIVE TIME: 1 HOUR

COOK TIME: 25 TO 30 MINUTES

FOR THE DOUGH

Olive oil, for greasing

¼ cup warm water

2½ teaspoons active dry yeast

½ cup granulated sugar, plus a pinch

½ cup whole milk

1 stick salted butter

Pinch sea salt

1 egg, lightly beaten

3½ cups all-purpose flour, divided, plus more for kneading

FOR THE FILLING

1 stick salted butter, melted

½ cup dark brown sugar

½ cup light brown sugar

2 tablespoons ground cinnamon

1 teaspoon vanilla extract

1 cup chopped pecans

FOR THE ICING

1 cup powdered sugar

1 teaspoon vanilla extract

3 tablespoons water

1. Coat a large bowl with olive oil and set aside.

2. In another large bowl, whisk the water, yeast, and a pinch of sugar u yeast dissolves.

3. In a small saucepan over low heat, combine the milk and butter, and until the butter melts. Remove from the heat and whisk into the yeas mixture.

4. Add the remaining ½ cup of sugar, salt, egg, and 2 cups of flour. Stir to combine.

5. Add the remaining 1½ cups of flour, ½ cup at a time, and stir until it f a dough. Turn the dough out onto a floured work surface (or silicone baking mat), adding flour as needed to keep the dough workable, an knead for 5 minutes.

6. Transfer the dough to the oiled bowl, turn once, and cover loosely wi kitchen towel. Allow the dough to rise in a warm place for 1 hour.

7. While the dough is rising, combine the melted butter, light and dark b sugar, cinnamon, vanilla, and pecans in a medium mixing bowl. Stir mix.

8. Preheat the oven to 350°F.

9. When the dough has risen, turn it out onto a floured work surface an into a 12 × 16" rectangle about ½-inch thick.

10. Spread the filling evenly over the dough.

11. Starting at the long side, roll the dough onto itself to form a tight log. the dough into 8 equal slices and arrange them in your skillet, cut-sid

12. Bake for 25 to 30 minutes or until bubbling and golden brown.

13. While the rolls are baking, in a small bowl, whisk together the powde sugar, vanilla, and water. Drizzle the rolls with icing immediately after come out of the oven.

Substitution tip: For a gluten-free version, I use King Arthur's all-purpose gluten-free flour blend. It's the best. When making this swap, be sure to also increase the amount of liquid, using 1 cup of milk instead of a ½ cup.

Iced Lemon Scones

VEGETARIAN

Like many other Americans, I have become obsessed with The Great British Baking Show. I love that it is kind, I love that the contestants are supportive, I love that they say words like stodgy, and I love how they pronounce oregano. It always leaves me hungry, and it has inspired me to try my hand at recipes I normally wouldn't, such as an Easter pavlova and a variety of scones. These particular scones are a classic—lemon and a simple icing—and they're lovely. They're the perfect treat to nibble on while you listen to Mary Berry politely rip someone apart.

SERVES 8
PREP TIME: 20 MINUTES
COOK TIME: 25 TO 30 MINUTES

3 cups all-purpose flour

½ teaspoon baking soda

2 teaspoons baking powder

½ cup sugar

¼ teaspoon salt

1 stick cold salted butter, cubed

1 cup buttermilk

2 egg yolks

1 tablespoon lemon zest

FOR THE ICING

1 cup powdered sugar

Juice of 1 lemon

1. In a large bowl, sift together the flour, baking soda, baking powder, s and salt.

2. Add the butter and, using your hands, work it into the flour mixture. T finished texture should resemble cornmeal.

3. In a small bowl, combine the buttermilk, egg yolks, and lemon zest. P the wet mixture into the dry mixture and stir together with a wooden until a loose dough forms.

4. Turn the dough out onto a floured surface and, working carefully so a to overmix, form a circle. Slice the dough into 8 even triangles.

5. Heat your skillet over medium-low heat. Gently place 4 triangles on t skillet. Cook for 6 to 8 minutes until the scones begin to brown and ri Flip and cook for an additional 6 to 8 minutes.

6. Repeat until all the scones are cooked, transferring them to a cooling as they come off the skillet.

7. Whisk together the powdered sugar and lemon juice and drizzle over warm scones before serving.

Menu-planning tip: Freeze the dough triangles raw and then simply bake them in your skillet in a 400°F oven for 30 to 35 minutes.

Masa Harina Cornbread

VEGETARIAN

Truly gluten-free cornbread is tricky to pull off, since it is frequently too dry or crumbly. But a hearty dose of buttermilk and butter helps this cornbread keep that much-desired moistness while staying naturally gluten-free.

SERVES 4

PREP TIME: 15 MINUTES

COOK TIME: 20 MINUTES

2½ cups masa harina

1½ teaspoons sea salt

2 teaspoons baking powder

1 teaspoon baking soda

2 cups buttermilk

6 tablespoons salted butter, melted, plus more for brushing the skillet and serving

1 egg

Honey, for drizzling

1. Preheat the oven to 400°F. Place your skillet in the oven on the midd rack.

2. In a large bowl, stir together the masa harina, salt, baking powder, a baking soda.

3. In a small bowl, whisk the buttermilk, butter, and egg.

4. Remove the skillet from the oven and brush with butter. Pour the bat into the hot skillet and return the pan to the oven.

5. Bake for 20 minutes or until the cornbread is cooked through and bro on top.

6. Serve with softened butter and a drizzle of honey.

> Substitution tip: Add 1 minced jalapeño to the batter for a spicy twist!

English Muffins

VEGETARIAN

What I love most about English muffins, besides the fact that they give me an excuse to use the word craggy, is how they are the perfect vehicle for salted butter or creamy peanut butter. They melt down into the cracks and fill your mouth with flavor as you bite into unexpected pockets. Homemade English muffins come together easily, and they're ideal for making in advance: The longer you let the dough rise in the refrigerator, the better they are.

SERVES 12
PREP TIME: 25 MINUTES
INACTIVE TIME: 2 HOURS 40 MINUTES
COOK TIME: 30 TO 35 MINUTES

1 teaspoon olive oil, for greasing

1 teaspoon dry active yeast

1 cup milk, room temperature

2 tablespoons salted butter, melted, plus more for skillet (optional)

2 tablespoons sugar

3 cups all-purpose flour

1 teaspoon sea salt

½ cup semolina

1. Coat a large bowl with olive oil and set aside.

2. In another large bowl, whisk together the yeast, milk, butter, and sug sit for 10 minutes. Add in the flour and salt, and stir to combine.

3. Turn the dough out onto a floured surface and knead for 10 to 12 mi until a soft ball forms. (Alternately, knead with a dough hook on a sta mixer for 5 to 7 minutes.)

4. Transfer the dough to the oiled bowl, turn once, and cover lightly with towel. Allow the dough to rise in a warm place for 1½ hours, until the dough has doubled in size.

5. Turn the dough out onto a floured surface and divide it into 12 equal pieces.

6. Gently roll each piece into a ball, working carefully to retain the bubb the dough.

7. Sprinkle a baking sheet with half the semolina and place the dough r on top. Sprinkle the dough with the remaining semolina and allow to an additional hour in a warm place.

8. If the patina on your skillet is well oiled, this recipe doesn't need any additional cooking fat. If you are still building the patina, melt 1 tables of butter in your skillet to coat it and prevent sticking.

9. Heat the skillet over medium heat. Place 4 muffins on the hot skillet cook for 5 to 6 minutes, until the bottoms have browned. Flip and co additional 5 to 6 minutes, adjusting the heat as necessary to prevent burning.

10. As the muffins are done, transfer them to a cooling rack. Repeat with remaining rounds, adding butter to the skillet as needed between bat to prevent sticking.

Ingredient tip: For a craggier, more complex dough, allow it to rise in the refrigerator overnight.

Pull-Apart Garlic Knots

VEGETARIAN

Garlic knots are a truly wonderful comfort food. They are irresistibly good, with more butter and garlic than any one piece of bread really deserves to have. When piping hot, they have a melt-in-your-mouth quality that makes it very, very difficult to not eat the whole skillet. Which is to say, they're a great party snack, but there's also no shame in having a date with Netflix and a skillet full of goodness.

SERVES 4 TO 6

PREP TIME: 20 MINUTES

INACTIVE TIME: 1 HOUR 25 MINUTES

COOK TIME: 25 TO 30 MINUTES

FOR THE DOUGH

1½ tablespoons olive oil, plus more for greasing

1 tablespoon dry active yeast

1 tablespoon sea salt

¾ cup warm water

2½ cups bread flour, plus more for kneading

FOR THE GLAZE

1 stick salted butter, melted

1 teaspoon sea salt

3 garlic cloves, minced

FOR THE TOPPING

½ cup grated Parmesan cheese

1 tablespoon dried oregano

1. Coat a large bowl with olive oil and set aside.

2. In another large bowl, whisk together 1½ tablespoons of olive oil, the yeast, salt, and water. Whisk until fully incorporated and frothing. Let 10 minutes.

3. Add half the flour and stir the mixture with a wooden spoon. Add the remaining flour and use your hands to knead everything together. Kn for 10 minutes, until the dough ball is smooth and pliable.

4. Transfer the dough to the oiled bowl, turn once, and cover lightly with towel. Allow the dough to rise in a warm place for 1 hour, until the do has doubled in size.

5. Punch the dough down and allow it to rise for 15 more minutes.

6. Heat the oven to 400°F.

7. Gently turn the dough out onto a floured surface. Knead for 5 to 7 mi until the dough is pliable and stretches nicely without tearing.

8. Divide the dough into 16 even pieces. Roll each piece out into a 6" cylinder, adding flour as needed to keep the dough from sticking.

9. Tie each cylinder into a simple knot, tucking the ends under the botto and arranging them in your skillet so they sit snugly next to each oth

10. In a small bowl, mix together the melted butter, salt, and garlic. Brus knots generously with the garlic butter. Top with the Parmesan and oregano.

11. Bake for 25 to 30 minutes, until the knots rise and are golden brown.

12. Allow to cool slightly before serving.

Menu-planning tip: These are irresistible on their own but also very, very good when served with a marinara dipping sauce.

Rosemary and Garlic Focaccia

VEGAN

The skillet is truly the perfect tool for obtaining well-made, crisp on all the edges, focaccia. Good focaccia should be crunchy, soft, full of flavor, and dripping with olive oil. This low-fuss bread is easy to throw together and a delicious addition to a meal.

SERVES 4 TO 6

PREP TIME: 20 MINUTES

INACTIVE TIME: 2 HOURS

COOK TIME: 25 MINUTES

1 cup warm water

1 tablespoon dry active yeast

6 tablespoons olive oil, divided

1 teaspoon sea salt, divided

2½ cups all-purpose flour

3 garlic cloves

1 tablespoon coarsely chopped rosemary

1. Coat a large bowl with olive oil and set aside.

2. In another large bowl, mix together the water, yeast, 2 tablespoons o oil, and ½ teaspoon of salt. Let the mixture sit for 10 minutes.

3. Add the flour, a little at a time, stirring with a wooden spoon.

4. When a rough ball has formed, turn it out onto a floured surface. Kne until the dough is pliable and smooth, 10 to 12 minutes.

5. Transfer the dough to the oiled bowl, turn once, and cover lightly with towel. Allow the dough to rise in a warm place for 1 hour, until the do has doubled in size.

6. Punch down the dough. Coat your skillet with 2 tablespoons of olive roll the dough into a 12" round. Place in the skillet and cover with a t Allow the dough to rise another 40 to 45 minutes.

7. Heat the oven to 400°F.

8. Use your fingers to dimple the dough. Top with the remaining olive oi garlic, rosemary, and salt.

9. Bake until the focaccia is a light golden brown, about 25 minutes.

10. Allow to cool slightly before serving.

Menu-planning tip: Focaccia is a delight when served warm with olive oil for dipping. It also makes a very good sandwich bread. My personal favorite combination is roasted turkey, provolone cheese, and pesto.

Buttermilk Biscuits

VEGETARIAN

After our son was born, we realized how having a new baby can be like a bomb going off in your social life. Friends we once saw frequently faded back into the rafters, and getting out of the house was more complicated than ever before. We recovered from the shock of growing our family, eventually, but not without serious effort to make our lives balanced. One of the ways that we made socializing work in our new family landscape was to host a monthly potluck brunch, an open-invitation event where friends could show up and share a meal and some time together. We'd always make biscuits, and each month there was a different cast of characters around our table. It has been one of the loveliest things we've done, and I still cherish the memories and connections we made.

SERVES 6

PREP TIME: 10 MINUTES

COOK TIME: 20 TO 25 MINUTES

2 cups all-purpose flour, plus more for kneading

1 teaspoon baking soda

2 teaspoons baking powder

1 teaspoon sea salt

1 stick cold salted butter, plus more for greasing

1 cup buttermilk

1. Heat the oven to 425°F.

2. In a medium bowl, mix the flour, baking soda, baking powder, and sa

3. Add the stick of butter in cubes to the flour mixture. Mix together with hands, crumbling until the texture resembles coarse cornmeal.

4. Stir in the buttermilk.

5. Grease your skillet with butter.

6. On a floured work surface, pat the dough out into a large rectangle. the dough in half and turn; pat it out again into a large rectangle. Rep this process 3 to 4 times, folding the dough in half and rotating each Add flour as you work to keep the dough from sticking.

7. Pat the dough out to 1½ to 2" thickness. Use a 3" biscuit cutter (or ja to cut the biscuits into rounds.

8. Arrange the rounds in the skillet so they are nice and snug. (This hel with rise!)

9. Bake for 20 to 25 minutes or until cooked through and golden brown.

Skill-building tip: For "sample size" biscuits, cut them into 1" cubes before baking. These are perfect for sliders.

Pita Bread

VEGAN

As a sandwich vessel, pita is hard to beat. But that's just one of this bread's many uses. Pita is also delicious freshly made and dipped in garlicky hummus or as the base of a quick pizza. It's versatile, it's tasty, and it's simple to make in your skillet.

SERVES 8
PREP TIME: 20 MINUTES
INACTIVE TIME: 1 HOUR 30 MINUTES
COOK TIME: 25 MINUTES

1 cup warm water

2 teaspoons dry active yeast

½ teaspoon sugar

2 teaspoons sea salt

3 cups all-purpose flour, plus more for kneading

1 tablespoon olive oil, plus more for greasing

1. Coat a large bowl with olive oil and set aside.

2. In a mixing bowl, combine the water, yeast, and sugar. Stir well and l mixture sit for 10 minutes.

3. Add the salt and slowly work in the flour, a little at a time, with a woo spoon.

4. When a rough dough ball has formed, turn it out onto a floured surfa Knead for 7 to 10 minutes, until the dough is smooth and elastic.

5. Transfer the dough to the oiled bowl, turn once, and cover lightly with towel. Allow the dough to rise in a warm place for 1 hour, until the do has doubled in size.

6. Gently punch down the dough and turn it out onto a floured work sur Divide it into 8 equal pieces. Cover loosely with a towel and let it rest minutes.

7. Gently form the pieces into discs, about 8" across and ¼" thick. Add flour to the dough as you work it to avoid sticking.

8. Heat your skillet over medium-high heat. Add a little oil to the pan, an when the skillet is hot, cook your pitas one at a time. Cook for 1½ mi per side, allowing the dough to puff up and brown.

9. Transfer to a rack to cool and repeat with the remaining dough. Add the skillet between each pita to avoid sticking.

Menu-planning tip: Pita keeps well in the refrigerator, so it's ideal to make a batch and use it throughout the week for lunches.

Sesame Broccoli

CHAPTER 4: Skillet Sides

Balsamic Brussels Sprouts with Mozzarella and Pecans
Crispy Sweet Potatoes
Spicy Black Beans with Cotija
Lemon and Parmesan Asparagus
Parmesan and Parsley Smashed Potatoes
Roasted Cabbage
Sesame Broccoli
Elote
Roasted Red Potatoes
Hash Browns
Twice-Baked Potatoes
Roasted Root Vegetables
Collards and Black-Eyed Peas
Zucchini and Tomato Gratin
Tostones

Balsamic Brussels Sprouts with Mozzarella and Pecans

VEGETARIAN

Can you think of a vegetable that has had a more enviable (and well deserved) comeback than Brussels sprouts? Once scorned by many as gross, these humble cruciferous sprouts have returned in a blaze of glory and bacon to steal the show and prove to everyone that, actually, they're amazing—just as long as you don't boil them. You can sauté and roast them in the same cast-iron skillet, offering a supersmooth stove-to-oven transfer, not to mention great flavor. And although I love Brussels sprouts prepared many different ways, my current favorite is to roast them with a bit of balsamic and then toss them with mozzarella and toasted pecans. The combination is sweet and earthy, crispy and soft, lovely on its own or alongside a roast or a chicken breast.

SERVES 2 TO 4

PREP TIME: 10 MINUTES

COOK TIME: 40 TO 45 MINUTES

24 Brussels sprouts, trimmed and halved

1 tablespoon olive oil

1 teaspoon sea salt

1 tablespoon balsamic vinegar, plus a drizzle to finish

2 garlic cloves, minced

1 tablespoon butter

½ cup pecans, coarsely chopped

1 cup cubed fresh mozzarella

1. Preheat the oven to 350°F.

2. In your skillet, toss the Brussels sprouts with the olive oil, salt, balsa vinegar, and garlic.

3. Roast in the oven for 40 to 45 minutes, until the Brussels sprouts are tender.

4. While the sprouts are roasting, melt the butter in a small pan over m high heat. Add the pecans and, stirring frequently, cook for 2 to 3 min until toasted. Remove from the heat and set aside.

5. Transfer the Brussels sprouts to a bowl, and mix in the pecans and mozzarella. Drizzle with balsamic. Serve warm.

Menu-planning tip: My trusty recipe tester said the only thing that would make this better was a bit of bacon!

Crispy Sweet Potatoes

VEGAN → QUICK AND EASY

Crispy sweet potatoes are one of the foods in my "always a hit" parenting bag of tricks. My son will always eat them, which means they're a go-to choice for lunches and family meals. They're incredibly versatile—delicious on their own but also wonderful in tacos, quesadillas, with eggs, or served as a side dish.

SERVES 2 TO 4

PREP TIME: 5 MINUTES

COOK TIME: 10 TO 15 MINUTES

1 large sweet potato

2 tablespoons coconut oil

1 teaspoon chipotle powder

1 teaspoon sea salt

1. Peel and cube the sweet potato into ½" squares.

2. In your skillet, melt the coconut oil over medium-high heat.

3. Add the sweet potato to the skillet in an even layer. Sprinkle with half chipotle powder and half the salt.

4. Cook for 6 to 7 minutes, until the sweet potato has browned and beg soften.

5. Flip the potatoes, sprinkle on the remaining chipotle powder and salt cook for another 4 to 5 minutes, until the potatoes are soft, cooked through, and crisp around the edges.

6. Remove from the heat and serve warm.

Menu-planning tip: Top with a fried egg for an easy and fast breakfast.

Spicy Black Beans with Cotija

VEGETARIAN → QUICK AND EASY

Spicy black beans work their way into a lot of recipes in our house. We eat them with huevos rancheros, tacos, tostadas, chilaquiles, and on their own. Like crispy sweet potatoes, these are a forever hit with my son, so they make their way into lunch boxes and breakfast plates. They're simple but hearty, full of flavor, and something we come back to over and over.

SERVES 2 TO 4
PREP TIME: 10 MINUTES
COOK TIME: 15 MINUTES

1 tablespoon olive oil

1 yellow onion, minced

3 garlic cloves, minced

1 jalapeño pepper, seeded and minced

2 (15-ounce) cans black beans, drained

½ cup vegetable stock

1 teaspoon salt

½ teaspoon ground cumin

½ teaspoon chipotle powder

¼ teaspoon cayenne

Juice of 1 lime

¼ cup cotija cheese, crumbled

¼ cup fresh cilantro, coarsely chopped

1. In your skillet, heat the oil over medium heat.

2. Sauté the onion and garlic for 2 to 3 minutes, until softened. Add the jalapeño pepper and cook for another minute.

3. Add the black beans, vegetable stock, salt, cumin, chipotle, and caye Stir well to combine and reduce the heat to low.

4. Simmer for 10 minutes, stirring frequently.

5. Remove from the heat and stir in the lime juice. Top with the cotija an cilantro to serve.

Menu-planning tip: Make a simple meal out of this dish by combining black beans, sweet potatoes, half an avocado, and a squeeze of lime juice.

Lemon and Parmesan Asparagus

VEGETARIAN → QUICK AND EASY

There is no vegetable that captures the relief and anticipation of spring like asparagus. After a long, cold, miserable winter, there is finally, finally, a fresh vegetable that hasn't been stored all winter or shipped from a different hemisphere. Finally, the promise that things will thaw, food will grow, and warmth will return.

SERVES 2 TO 4

PREP TIME: 5 MINUTES

COOK TIME: 10 MINUTES

2 tablespoons salted butter

2 pounds asparagus, woody ends trimmed

Juice of 1 lemon

Pinch sea salt

¼ cup grated Parmesan cheese

1. In your skillet, melt the butter over medium heat.

2. Put the asparagus in the pan and toss to coat with butter. Cover with

3. Cook for 3 to 4 minutes, then turn the asparagus. Re-cover and cook an additional 3 to 4 minutes, until the asparagus is bright green.

4. Transfer to a plate and top with the lemon juice, salt, and Parmesan. warm.

Ingredient tip: Asparagus is easily overcooked, and that is a travesty. Keep a close eye on it, and pull it off the heat as soon as it is a bright green.

Parmesan and Parsley Smashed Potatoes

VEGETARIAN

Smashed potatoes take slightly more effort than your average roasted potato, but the payoff is huge and absolutely worth it. They are crispy, buttery, garlicky, and the best companion to a Perfect Cast-Iron Steak. Bonus: Your cast-iron skillet is heavy enough to withstand in-pan potato smashing so you can quickly return the spuds to the oven.

SERVES 2 TO 4

PREP TIME: 10 MINUTES

COOK TIME: 1 HOUR 15 MINUTES

7 to 10 small or medium red potatoes

¼ cup olive oil, divided

1 teaspoon sea salt, divided

1 teaspoon red pepper flakes, divided

4 tablespoons salted butter, cubed

2 garlic cloves, minced

½ cup grated Parmesan cheese

¼ cup curly parsley, minced

1. Preheat the oven to 350°F.

2. In your skillet, toss the potatoes with 2 tablespoons of olive oil, ½ tea of salt, and ½ teaspoon of red pepper flakes.

3. Transfer the skillet to the oven and roast the potatoes for 30 minutes until a fork easily penetrates the potatoes.

4. Remove the skillet and increase the oven temperature to 425°F.

5. Use a fork or meat tenderizer to smash the potatoes flat. Return the the oven and roast for 25 minutes.

6. Remove the skillet from the oven. Flip the potatoes and top with the remaining olive oil, salt, red pepper flakes, and the butter, garlic, and Parmesan cheese.

7. Roast for 15 to 20 more minutes, until cooked through, brown, and c

8. Top with the parsley and serve hot.

Time-saving tip: The first roast can be completed ahead of time; just add a few minutes onto the second roast to account for refrigeration.

Roasted Cabbage

VEGAN → QUICK AND EASY

Roasted cabbage is one of the more versatile vegetables in our meal planning. I love it as a side for different meats, stirred into mashed potatoes, or dressed up in a warm salad. Roasting cabbage makes it slightly sweet while keeping the crunch and adding a little bit of char.

SERVES 2 TO 4

PREP TIME: 5 MINUTES

COOK TIME: 20 MINUTES

1 small head white cabbage

1 tablespoon olive oil

Pinch sea salt

Pinch red pepper flakes

2 tablespoons apple cider vinegar (optional)

1. Heat the oven to 400°F.

2. Halve the cabbage and then slice each half into ½"-thick strips.

3. In your skillet, toss the cabbage with the olive oil, salt, and red peppe flakes. Spread the cabbage evenly across the bottom of the skillet.

4. Roast in the oven for 15 minutes, stir, and then roast for an additiona 5 minutes.

5. Finish with the apple cider vinegar (if using) to serve.

> Menu-planning tip: Roasted cabbage is a frequent part of my make-ahead lunches. I roast a head of cabbage and braise a week's worth of chicken thighs.

Lunch is a healthy serving of cabbage and a chicken thigh with either barbecue sauce or a citrusy vinaigrette.

Sesame Broccoli

VEGAN → QUICK AND EASY

When Dan and I first started dating, he had a laundry list of vegetables he wasn't sure he liked or didn't particularly care to try. Over the years we've worked our way through the list, and I'm proud to say that I've won him over on most of them. One such win was broccoli, a vegetable that we have both come to love most with a little char on it from the skillet. Tossed in a simple sesame sauce, this broccoli is the perfect side to a number of different main dishes, or lovely eaten alone with a serving of rice.

SERVES 2 TO 4
PREP TIME: 5 MINUTES
COOK TIME: 10 MINUTES

4 tablespoons sesame oil, divided

1 head broccoli, separated into florets and halved

1 tablespoon soy sauce

3 garlic cloves, minced

1. In your skillet, heat 2 tablespoons of sesame oil over medium-high h

2. Put the broccoli in the hot skillet, evenly distributing it across the bott Cook for 2 to 3 minutes without turning.

3. Flip the broccoli and add the soy sauce, remaining sesame oil, and g Cover and cook for another 2 to 3 minutes.

4. Serve warm.

> Substitution tip: We also love this recipe with broccolini, particularly because the stalks also get a nice char.

Elote

VEGETARIAN → QUICK AND EASY

Elote, also known as Mexican street corn, is grilled or fried fresh corn on the cob slathered in mayonnaise or crema, cotija cheese, and cayenne, topped with lime juice, and served hot. It's one of my favorite appetizers and pairs perfectly with a dinner of Black Bean and Avocado Tostadas and margaritas.

SERVES 4
PREP TIME: 15 MINUTES
COOK TIME: 20 MINUTES

4 ears corn, shucked

2 tablespoons olive oil

½ cup mayonnaise

¾ cup crumbled cotija cheese, divided

½ teaspoon sea salt

1 teaspoon chipotle powder

1 garlic clove, minced

½ teaspoon cayenne

½ cup fresh cilantro, minced

1 lime, quartered

1. Brush the corn with olive oil on all sides.

2. Heat your skillet over medium-high heat. Add the corn to the hot pan turning every 3 to 4 minutes. Cook for 17 to 20 minutes, until all side slightly blackened and the corn kernels are bright yellow.

3. While the corn is cooking, mix the mayonnaise, ½ cup of cotija, salt, chipotle, and garlic. Spread it out in a thick layer on a large plate.

4. When the corn is done, roll each ear in the mayonnaise mixture. Top corn with the remaining cotija, cayenne, and cilantro, being sure to tu evenly coat each side.

5. Serve warm with a lime wedge.

Substitution tip: For a less-spicy take on this dish, try paprika instead of cayenne.

Roasted Red Potatoes

VEGAN

Roasted red potatoes are a classic side dish that pairs well with almost every main course imaginable. We love them alongside steak, roasted chicken, or for brunch with a dippy egg and some beans. I also love the heavenly smell of potatoes roasting, thanks to the aromatic herbs and garlic.

SERVES 4 TO 6

PREP TIME: 20 MINUTES

COOK TIME: 30 TO 35 MINUTES

8 to 10 small to medium red potatoes, quartered

¼ cup olive oil

1 teaspoon sea salt

3 garlic cloves, minced

1 tablespoon coarsely chopped fresh rosemary

1 tablespoon coarsely chopped fresh oregano

1. Heat the oven to 400°F.
2. In your skillet, combine the potatoes, olive oil, salt, garlic, rosemary, oregano and toss to evenly coat.
3. Roast in the oven for 20 minutes, give the potatoes a good stir, and r for another 10 to 15 minutes until cooked through and crisp.
4. Serve warm.

> Ingredient tip: I love to slice up a parsnip and throw it in with my red potatoes for an extra dose of earthy root veggies.

Hash Browns

VEGAN → QUICK AND EASY

I love having breakfast for dinner. It's not often we cook a full breakfast spread in the morning, so "brinner" is our chance to pull out all the stops. Usually this involves some sort of breakfast meat, eggs fried to perfection (see here), and a big skillet full of hash browns. There's something magical about crispy-all-over potatoes and runny egg yolk.

SERVES 4
PREP TIME: 15 MINUTES
COOK TIME: 10 TO 15 MINUTES

1 large russet potato, grated

1 small white onion, chopped

2 garlic cloves, minced

1 teaspoon sea salt

¼ teaspoon red pepper flakes

1 tablespoon olive oil

1. Place the grated potatoes in a large kitchen towel. Over the sink, wri towel to squeeze the excess liquid out of the potatoes.

2. In a large bowl, combine the potatoes, onion, garlic, salt, and red pe flakes.

3. In your skillet, heat the oil over medium-high heat.

4. Spread the potato mixture evenly over the bottom of the hot skillet.

5. Cook for 5 to 8 minutes without stirring, until the potatoes have beco deep golden brown. Use a spatula to gently free the potatoes and flip

6. Cook for an additional 5 to 8 minutes, until the potatoes are brown al

> Menu-planning tip: If what you're looking for are hash brown patties, try the Classic Latkes.

Twice-Baked Potatoes

Twice-baked potatoes taste like childhood to me. One bite, and I am instantly transported to the house where I grew up, standing in the kitchen with my siblings, each adding a topping as we slid the potatoes down an assembly line. Like so many potato dishes, twice-baked potatoes are a blank slate where you can go wild with your favorite toppings and combinations. I've suggested some of mine, but feel free to dream big!

SERVES 4

PREP TIME: 15 MINUTES

COOK TIME: 1 HOUR 20 MINUTES

4 large russet potatoes

1 tablespoon olive oil

1 cup mayonnaise

3 tablespoons butter, room temperature

4 ounces bacon, cooked and chopped

1 teaspoon sea salt

1 cup shredded cheddar cheese

⅓ cup minced scallions

1. Heat the oven to 375°F.

2. Poke each potato with a fork to create holes on each side. Put the potatoes in your skillet and drizzle with the olive oil.

3. Bake the potatoes for 1 hour.

4. Remove the potatoes from the oven and let cool. When they are coo enough to handle, slice each potato in half lengthwise. Scoop the fle a large bowl. Set the skins aside.

5. Add the mayonnaise, butter, bacon, and salt to the cooked potato. M until creamy.

6. Evenly distribute the mashed potatoes into the four potato skins. Top the cheese.

7. Return the stuffed potatoes to the skillet and bake for an additional 2 minutes, until the cheese is melted and bubbling.

8. Top with the scallions before serving.

Fun tip: Twice-baked potatoes are a delightful party food. Let guests assemble their own from a buffet of toppings: cilantro, cheddar cheese, bacon, scallions, roasted mushrooms, bell peppers, red onions, blue cheese, sour cream, chipotle aioli, minced jalapeños, and corn.

Roasted Root Vegetables

VEGAN

For me, roasted root vegetables are as symbolic of winter as asparagus is of spring. They feel warm and comforting, like snuggling up for the long cold months and eating by the fire.

SERVES 4
PREP TIME: 15 MINUTES
COOK TIME: 40 TO 45 MINUTES

1 large purple beet, peeled and cubed

1 large golden beet, peeled and cubed

1 sweet potato, peeled and cubed

5 small red potatoes, quartered

1 parsnip, peeled and cubed

5 carrots, peeled and sliced

1 yellow onion, diced

¼ cup olive oil

1 tablespoon herbes de Provence

3 garlic cloves, minced

1 teaspoon sea salt

1. Heat the oven to 400°F.

2. In your skillet, combine the beets, potatoes, parsnip, carrots, and oni with the olive oil, herbes de Provence, garlic, and salt. Mix well to co spread the vegetables evenly over the skillet bottom.

3. Roast in the oven for 25 minutes, stir well, and roast for an additiona 20 minutes. When the vegetables are cooked through and browning around the edges, remove from the heat.

4. Stir well to distribute the juices before serving.

> Substitution tip: Root vegetables are a lovely base for herbs and spices. Fresh herbs are a great addition, but I also love this dish with curry, turmeric, and a dash of cayenne.

Collards and Black-Eyed Peas

VEGETARIAN

A lot of foods remind me of my dad, because our relationship was rooted deeply in a mutual love of cooking and eating. But without a doubt, one food that brings him vividly to mind every time I make it is collards with black-eyed peas. It's a simple dish grounded in generations of Southern history, and although it is eaten throughout the fall, winter, and spring, it has strong ties to New Year's traditions. My father was absolute in his belief that eating this dish (alongside pork) on New Year's Day would bring a year of prosperity and luck, and this is a tradition that I will hold to in his honor for the rest of my days.

SERVES 4

PREP TIME: 15 MINUTES

INACTIVE TIME: 4 HOURS (OR OVERNIGHT)

COOK TIME: 40 MINUTES

1 cup black-eyed peas, soaked

2 tablespoons salted butter

1 white onion, diced

3 garlic cloves, minced

1 bunch collard greens, ribbed and thinly sliced

½ teaspoon salt

1 tablespoon apple cider vinegar

¼ teaspoon red pepper flakes

1. Soak the peas for at least 4 hours before cooking—or overnight—in water. Drain and rinse.

2. In your skillet, melt the butter over medium heat.

3. Sauté the onion, stirring frequently, for 3 to 4 minutes. Add the garlic collard greens to the pan. Stir occasionally to coat and cook for anot to 4 minutes.

4. Add the black-eyed peas, salt, vinegar, and red pepper flakes. Stir w reduce the heat to low.

5. Cook for 20 to 25 minutes, stirring occasionally, until the beans have softened.

6. Season to taste before serving.

Ingredient tip: If you're looking to secure all your New Year's fortune in one dish, add in bacon with the onions.

Zucchini and Tomato Gratin

VEGETARIAN → QUICK AND EASY

This simple summer gratin is a lovely showcase of two warm weather vegetables. It comes together easily and without fuss, and the stars of the show truly shine together.

SERVES 4

PREP TIME: 10 MINUTES

COOK TIME: 20 TO 25 MINUTES

2 large ripe tomatoes, cut into ¼" slices

1 large zucchini, cut into ¼" slices

¼ cup olive oil

3 garlic cloves, minced

1 cup grated Parmesan cheese

½ teaspoon sea salt

1 tablespoon fresh oregano, minced

1 tablespoon fresh thyme, minced

1. Heat the oven to 375°F.

2. In your skillet, arrange the tomatoes and the zucchini in alternating r overlapping a little so they stand up.

3. Drizzle with the olive oil and top with the garlic.

4. In a small bowl, mix together the Parmesan, salt, oregano, and thym Sprinkle the mixture over the top of the vegetables.

5. Bake for 20 to 25 minutes, until the zucchini is cooked through and t cheese has formed a golden crust.

6. Serve warm.

> Ingredient tip: To make this a heartier dish, add thinly sliced red potatoes.

Tostones

VEGETARIAN → QUICK AND EASY

Fried plantains are one of my favorite foods. They're incredibly simple and yet packed with flavor. Tostones are slightly more complicated but also deliver on flavor and texture. Served with a simple avocado-lime crema, these twice-fried plantains are a lovely combination of sweetness and acidity, cream, and crunch.

SERVES 2 TO 4
PREP TIME: 15 MINUTES
COOK TIME: 10 MINUTES

FOR THE TOSTONES

1 cup vegetable oil

2 green plantains, peeled and cut into ½" rounds

1 tablespoon salt

FOR THE SAUCE

2 avocados, peeled, pitted, and sliced

Juice of 2 limes

3 garlic cloves

1 cup Greek yogurt

1. In your skillet, heat the oil over medium-high heat to 375°F. Test the temperature of the oil by flicking a bit of water at it. If the water jumps around, the oil is ready.

2. Fry the plantains for 2 to 3 minutes, turning at least once, until they a golden and crisp.

3. Transfer to a baking rack and repeat until you've fried all the plantain Remove the pan from the heat and let the oil cool slightly, but do not discard it.

4. While the plantains are still warm, use a meat mallet or thick-bottome glass jar to flatten them to ¼" thickness.

5. Reheat the oil to 375°F. Fry the plantains a second time for 3 to 4 mi turning at least once, until they are a darker golden brown and crisp.

6. Transfer to a baking sheet and season with salt while they are still ho

7. In a food processor, combine the avocado, lime juice, garlic, and yog Blend until smooth.

8. Serve the warm tostones with the crema.

Ingredient tip: To try your hand at the once-fried plantain, cut ½" slices of plantain and fry for 2 to 3 minutes per side in melted butter. Top with a sprinkle of cinnamon and a drizzle of honey and enjoy.

Spinach and Ricotta Stuffed Shells

CHAPTER 5: Vegetarian Meals

Huevos Rancheros
Shakshuka
Fried Rice
Spinach and Mushroom Lasagna
Grilled Cheese
Sweet Potato Quesadilla
Classic Latkes
Falafel Salad
Cauliflower Steaks
Macaroni and Cheese
Black Bean Burger
Tempeh Taco Skillet
Black Bean and Avocado Tostadas
Spinach and Ricotta Stuffed Shells
Sesame Cauliflower

Huevos Rancheros

VEGETARIAN → QUICK AND EASY

Huevos rancheros are a staple in our weeknight dinner rotation. I'd wager that we've eaten them at least a few times a month for the past 10 years, and if that's not a winning endorsement of a recipe, I don't know what is. Occasionally we make them with refried beans instead of black beans, and depending on the season, we'll try different salsas. No matter what, we love the crisp tortilla, the runny egg, and the perfectly melted cheese.

SERVES 4

PREP TIME: 15 MINUTES

COOK TIME: 10 MINUTES

2 cups cherry tomatoes, quartered

1 jalapeño pepper, minced

½ red onion, chopped

2 garlic cloves, minced

½ bunch fresh cilantro, chopped

Salt and pepper

Juice of 2 limes

2 cups canned black beans, in their liquid

1 teaspoon red pepper flakes

1 tablespoon olive oil

4 corn tortillas

8 ounces cheddar cheese, grated and divided into 4 even portions, plus more for topping

4 eggs

1 large avocado, peeled, pitted, and sliced

1. In a mixing bowl, combine the tomatoes, jalapeño pepper, red onion, garlic, cilantro, a pinch of salt and pepper, and lime juice. Stir well an the salsa aside.

2. In a medium pot, cook the black beans and their liquid over medium Stir in the red pepper flakes and a pinch of salt and pepper.

3. In your skillet, heat the oil over medium heat.

4. Place a tortilla in the middle of your pan.

5. Make a ring around the edge of the tortilla using one portion of chee crack an egg into the center. Cook until the cheese has melted and t egg white has started to become opaque.

6. Use a spatula to cradle the tortilla, centered under the egg, and flip it quickly and confidently.

7. Cook for 2 to 3 minutes for a runny egg and 4 to 5 minutes for a firm Use the spatula to lift the tortilla and egg off the skillet and onto the p egg-side up.

8. Repeat with the remaining ingredients, reserving some cheese for to

9. Strain the black beans. Top each tortilla with black beans, avocado, and cheese.

Substitution tip: We love these with either ground beef or ground vegan meat cooked and mixed in with the beans.

Shakshuka

VEGETARIAN → ONE-SKILLET MEAL

Shakshuka has a storied past that winds through the Middle East, eventually becoming a staple in Israel, and for good reason. Eggs are gently poached in a richly spiced tomato sauce, and the whole dish is served with fresh pita. It's a wonderful way to start the day or a perfect answer to breakfast-for-dinner cravings.

SERVES 4

PREP TIME: 15 MINUTES

COOK TIME: 40 TO 45 MINUTES

1 tablespoon olive oil

1 white onion, chopped

3 garlic cloves, minced

1 jalapeño pepper, seeded and minced

2 tablespoons tomato paste

1 teaspoon smoked paprika

¼ teaspoon cayenne

1 teaspoon dried oregano

1 teaspoon ground cumin

1 teaspoon ground coriander

½ teaspoon sea salt

½ teaspoon freshly ground black pepper

1 (28-ounce) can diced tomatoes

½ cup vegetable broth, plus more if needed to thin sauce

4 eggs

¼ cup crumbled feta

Handful fresh parsley, chopped

Bread or pita, for serving

1. In your skillet, heat the oil over medium heat.

2. Add the onion, garlic, and jalapeño pepper to the pan. Cook for 5 to minutes, stirring frequently, until the onions begin to brown.

3. Stir in the tomato paste, paprika, cayenne, oregano, cumin, coriande and pepper. Stir well, working all the ingredients into the tomato past

4. After 1 to 2 minutes of stirring constantly, add the diced tomatoes an vegetable broth.

5. Stir well to incorporate all the ingredients, then reduce the heat to a simmer. Cook for 20 to 25 minutes.

6. Taste your sauce and adjust the seasoning to your liking. If it is too th (no liquid runs when you stir it), add another ¼ cup of vegetable brot water.

7. Crack the eggs into the sauce, cover the skillet, and increase the he medium.

8. Cook for 7 to 10 minutes for a soft yolk and 12 to 15 minutes for a fir yolk.

9. Remove from the heat and top with the feta and parsley. Serve hot w warm bread or pita.

Substitution tip: Try it served with Pita Bread or fresh challah for an Israeli-Jewish twist!

Fried Rice

VEGETARIAN → QUICK AND EASY → ONE-SKILLET MEAL

I would never lie to you and say this recipe is better than takeout because 80 percent of what's great about takeout is that you don't have to cook the food yourself. But I will tell you that this fried rice tastes wonderful and is packed full of vegetables and rich flavors. Plus, you can make a double batch and then eat the leftovers on your couch the next day, which is the best of both worlds.

SERVES 4
PREP TIME: 15 MINUTES
COOK TIME: 20 MINUTES

2 large eggs

Pinch sea salt

3 tablespoons peanut oil, divided

1 white onion, chopped

1 large carrot, shredded

2 garlic cloves, minced

1 cup shiitake mushrooms, sliced

½ cup chopped snow peas

1 cup chopped broccoli

1 tablespoon grated fresh ginger

¼ teaspoon red pepper flakes

1 tablespoon toasted sesame oil

3 cups cooked white rice

2 tablespoons soy sauce

¼ cup coarsely chopped scallions

1. In a small bowl, whisk the eggs together with a pinch of salt.

2. In your skillet, heat 1 teaspoon of oil over medium-high heat. Add the eggs, allowing them to coat the bottom of the skillet. Cook for 1 to 2 minutes, until they have begun to set. Use a spatula to free the eggs flip. Cook for an additional 2 to 3 minutes until cooked through.

3. Transfer the eggs to a medium bowl. Cover and place in the microwa keep warm.

4. Add 1 tablespoon of oil to the skillet and return it to the heat. Once th is hot, add the onion, carrot, and garlic to the skillet. Cook for 3 to 5 minutes, stirring occasionally, until the onions begin to brown.

5. While the onion mixture is cooking, coarsely chop the cooked eggs a return them to the bowl.

6. Add the mushrooms, snow peas, and broccoli to the pan. Cook for 3 minutes, until the vegetables begin to soften and brown. Remove the vegetables from the heat, mix them in with the eggs, and return the b the microwave.

7. Add the remaining oil to the pan and return to the heat. Add the ging pepper flakes, sesame oil, and rice to the skillet. Cook for 3 to 4 min stirring frequently, until the rice has warmed.

8. Return the vegetables and egg to the skillet and add the soy sauce. few times to combine and then remove the pan from the heat. Mix in scallions and taste to adjust the seasoning.

9. Serve immediately.

Substitution tip: Feel free to add whatever odd vegetables have been accumulating in your refrigerator. Just finely chop them and add them in at the end. Delicious!

Spinach and Mushroom Lasagna

VEGETARIAN

I feel very strongly that it is just as easy to make many lasagnas as it is to make just one, so I frequently find myself making three or more for both my family and others. Celebrating a birth? I'll make you a lasagna. Mourning a loss? Lasagna. Potluck dinner? I'm bringing lasagna. It's an all-occasion way for me to show my love. And in a cast-iron skillet, every piece is a corner piece.

SERVES 4 TO 6
PREP TIME: 15 MINUTES
COOK TIME: 1 HOUR 15 MINUTES

3 tablespoons olive oil, divided

1 white onion, chopped

4 garlic cloves, minced

1 (6-ounce) can tomato paste

1 (28-ounce) can diced tomatoes

1 teaspoon sea salt, divided

4 cups fresh spinach

2 cups cremini mushrooms, stemmed, cleaned, and sliced

2 cups ricotta cheese

1 egg

1 tablespoon dried oregano, divided

½ teaspoon freshly ground black pepper, divided

1 pound lasagna noodles

8 ounces fresh mozzarella, cut into ¼" slices

¼ teaspoon red pepper flakes

1 cup grated Parmesan cheese

1. In your skillet, heat 2 tablespoons of olive oil over medium heat.

2. Add the onion and garlic to the skillet and cook for 3 to 5 minutes, sti frequently, until the onion becomes translucent.

3. Add the tomato paste, stirring well to incorporate all the onion. Smea paste around the skillet to brown it, then add the diced tomatoes. Stir the tomato paste and the diced tomatoes fully incorporate, then add teaspoon of salt and reduce the heat to a simmer. Simmer for 20 to 2 minutes.

4. While the sauce is cooking, heat the remaining 1 tablespoon of olive another skillet over medium heat. Add the mushrooms and toss to co then spread evenly and cook for 3 to 5 minutes, stirring once and spreading them evenly again.

5. Add the garlic and spinach to the pan, working in batches if necessa to combine. Cook 2 to 3 minutes, stirring frequently, until the spinach wilted. Remove from the heat and transfer to a bowl.

6. Remove the pan from the heat and set aside ⅔ of the sauce.

7. Heat the oven to 400°F.

8. In a small bowl, whisk together the ricotta, egg, ½ tablespoon of oreg ½ teaspoon of salt, and ¼ teaspoon of black pepper.

9. Nestle a layer of noodles in the sauce left in the skillet. Top with half ricotta mixture. Add a layer of sauce and then a second layer of nood

10. Top the noodles with the spinach-and-mushroom mixture, followed b layer of mozzarella and then a layer of sauce.

11. Add a third layer of noodles. Top with the remaining ricotta mixture, spreading it evenly over the noodles. Follow with more sauce.

12. Add a fourth and final layer of noodles. Top with sauce, then finish wi remaining mozzarella, Parmesan, salt, pepper, and oregano.

13. Cover loosely with aluminum foil. Bake for 30 to 35 minutes, then re the foil and bake for an additional 10 minutes, until the cheese is mel and bubbling.

Menu-planning tip: Lasagna also freezes beautifully, so if you have room in your freezer, throw in a prebaked lasagna for later!

Grilled Cheese

VEGETARIAN → QUICK AND EASY → ONE-SKILLET MEAL

This is a classic. A staple. A dish that everyone should master. I've provided the basic method, but I encourage you to be bold! Experiment with different breads, different cheeses, and different fillings. There is no end to combinations that make for excellent grilled cheese, and this is definitely a dish where experimentation is heavily encouraged.

SERVES 2
PREP TIME: 5 MINUTES
COOK TIME: 10 MINUTES

3 tablespoons salted butter, room temperature, divided

4 slices thick, crusty bread

4 slices sharp cheddar cheese

1. In your skillet, melt 1 tablespoon of butter over medium-high heat.

2. Smear one side of each piece of bread with the remaining butter.

3. When the skillet is hot, for each sandwich, layer 1 piece of bread but side down, 2 slices of cheddar cheese, and a final piece of bread, bu side up.

4. Cook for 3 to 4 minutes, until the cheese has begun to melt and the has become golden brown. Flip. Cook for another 3 to 4 minutes, un bread is browned to your liking.

Substitution tip: One of my family's favorite grilled cheese twists is pairing thick crusty bread with a nice layer of fig jam, goat cheese, and arugula.

Sweet Potato Quesadilla

VEGETARIAN → QUICK AND EASY → ONE-SKILLET MEAL

Sometimes, especially on weeknights, I just need a dinner that is easy to make and I know everyone will eat happily. This hearty and filling dish is one of the options I keep in my back pocket. I love the combination of the soft sweet potatoes and the crispy tortilla. I serve it up with some beans, sour cream, and avocado slices and call it a dinner win.

SERVES 4
PREP TIME: 15 MINUTES
COOK TIME: 20 MINUTES

1 tablespoon coconut oil

1 small sweet potato, peeled and cubed

1 teaspoon chipotle powder

½ teaspoon sea salt

1 tablespoon olive oil, divided

8 tortillas

1 pound cheddar cheese, grated

¼ teaspoon red pepper flakes

1. In your skillet, melt the coconut oil over medium heat.

2. When the skillet is hot, add the sweet potatoes, chipotle, and salt. Co 10 to 12 minutes, stirring occasionally, until the sweet potatoes are c through and browned around the edges.

3. Transfer the potatoes to a bowl, wipe out the pan, and return it to the with a drizzle of olive oil.

4. On a cutting board near the skillet, layer 1 tortilla, ¼ the cheese, ¼ th sweet potatoes, a sprinkle of red pepper flakes, and a second tortilla Transfer to the skillet once the oil is hot.

5. Cook for 3 to 4 minutes, until the cheese has begun to melt and the t has crisped, and flip. Cook for an additional 3 to 4 minutes.

6. Transfer to the microwave to keep warm while you repeat with your remaining ingredients.

7. Slice each quesadilla into 4 to 6 even triangles before serving.

> Substitution tip: I use coconut oil to cook the sweet potatoes because I like the flavor it adds, but you can also use butter instead.

Classic Latkes

VEGETARIAN → QUICK AND EASY

Many years ago I worked as an educator at a Jewish museum with a woman named Esther. She was the Jewish grandmother I never had, and I delighted in her company. Each year we would have a public program called "Esther Fest" during Chanukah season, where she would demonstrate her famous latke method for a crowd of hungry fans. These days I lead a slightly different life as a Montessori preschool teacher, but every year during Chanukah, I break out my hot plate and show my students how to make Esther's latkes. They are always a big hit.

SERVES 4 TO 6

PREP TIME: 20 MINUTES

COOK TIME: 20 MINUTES

1 large russet potato, grated

1 small white onion, finely chopped

3 garlic cloves, minced

1 teaspoon sea salt

1 egg

½ cup vegetable oil

TO SERVE

Sour cream, for dipping

Applesauce, for dipping

1. Put the grated potato onto a large, clean dish towel and wring out the excess liquid over the sink.

2. In a medium bowl, combine the potato, onion, garlic, salt, and egg.

3. In your skillet, heat the oil over medium-high heat to 375°F.

4. When the oil is hot, use your hands to form a patty. It should be a littl smaller than the size of your palm. Gently place it in the oil, repeatin the skillet is full.

5. Cook for 3 to 4 minutes until sizzling and golden brown. Flip and coo another 3 to 4 minutes. When each latke is firm and golden brown, tr them to a plate in the microwave to keep warm.

6. Repeat with the remaining potato mixture.

7. Serve with a dollop of sour cream and applesauce for dipping.

Fun tip: I always have my students make Crock-Pot applesauce to go with the latkes, which is delightful and easy to make. Peel and slice 6 apples and combine in the Crock-Pot with 1 cup of water, the juice of 1 lemon, and 1 tablespoon of cinnamon. Cook overnight, about 10 hours, on low and mix to mash.

Falafel Salad

VEGETARIAN → QUICK AND EASY

Falafel is another food, like Esther's latkes, that I grew to love dearly in my time as a Jewish educator. There was even a time while we lived in Baltimore, I memorized the schedule of a falafel food truck and followed it around town. My family loves homemade falafel served up in fresh Pita Bread, but we also love them on top of a big, heaping salad where the hummus is the dressing and the warm falafel contrasts with the crisp, cool vegetables.

SERVES 4
PREP TIME: 15 MINUTES
COOK TIME: 20 MINUTES

FOR THE FALAFEL

2 (15-ounce) cans chickpeas, drained

4 garlic cloves, quartered

1 egg

1 teaspoon sea salt

1 white onion, sliced

½ cup all-purpose flour

1 teaspoon turmeric

1½ teaspoons ground cumin

½ teaspoon cayenne

¼ cup fresh parsley

½ cup vegetable oil

FOR THE TZATZIKI

1 cup Greek yogurt

Juice of 2 limes

¼ cup cilantro, minced

½ cucumber, finely chopped

FOR THE SALAD

8 cups arugula

½ cucumber, sliced

½ red onion, thinly sliced

½ cup crumbled feta

¼ cup roasted red peppers

12 cherry tomatoes, halved

¼ cup kalamata olives, halved

1 cup hummus

1 large lemon, quartered

2 tablespoons olive oil

1. In a food processor, combine the chickpeas, garlic, egg, salt, onion, f turmeric, cumin, cayenne, and parsley. Pulse, blending until smooth. (Check for chunks!)

2. In your skillet, heat the oil over medium-high heat to 375°F. Heat the to 200°F.

3. When the oil is hot, use a spoon to dollop the batter, 1 large tablespo at a time. Cook for 2 to 3 minutes, flip, and cook for another 2 to 3 m until the falafel is dark brown on both sides and firm.

4. Transfer to a sheet pan in the oven and repeat with the remaining ba

5. In a small bowl, combine the yogurt, lime juice, cilantro, and cucumb well.

6. Divide the arugula evenly between 4 plates. Distribute the cucumber onion, feta, red peppers, tomatoes, and kalamata olives.

7. Top each with falafel and a dollop of both tzatziki and hummus. Sque with lemon juice and drizzle with olive oil to serve.

> Menu-planning tip: These falafel balls are also delightful when combined in a warm pita with tzatziki, hummus, cucumbers, and onions.

Cauliflower Steaks

VEGAN → QUICK AND EASY → ONE-SKILLET MEAL

The past five years must have been a boon for cauliflower farmers. It's in everything now. And although I'll stick with pizza crust and rice prepared the old-fashioned way, I have to admit I've caught a little cauliflower fever. A cauliflower steak is a truly delightful way to enjoy this cruciferous vegetable, offering up char, crunch, and tenderness. And the decadent combination of butter, parsley, and garlic sends it over the top.

SERVES 2

PREP TIME: 5 MINUTES

COOK TIME: 20 MINUTES

¼ cup olive oil

1 head cauliflower, cut into ½"-thick slices

½ teaspoon sea salt

¼ teaspoon freshly ground black pepper

4 tablespoons butter, melted

1 cup fresh parsley, coarsely chopped

2 garlic cloves, minced

Juice of 1 lemon

1. Heat the oven to 375°F.

2. In your skillet, heat the olive oil over medium-high heat.

3. When the oil is hot, arrange the cauliflower steaks in the skillet and sprinkle with salt and pepper.

4. Cook for 2 to 3 minutes, then flip and cook for another 2 to 3 minutes

5. Transfer the skillet to the oven and bake for 10 to 12 minutes, until th cauliflower is cooked through and browned.

6. While the cauliflower is cooking, mix the butter, parsley, and garlic in small bowl.

7. When the cauliflower comes out of the oven, brush each steak with t butter mixture and top with a squeeze of lemon juice before serving.

> Substitution tip: For an umami-rich twist on the finishing sauce, try mixing together ¼ cup of soy sauce, ¼ cup of hoisin, 1 tablespoon of sesame oil, and 1 cup of chopped fresh cilantro.

Macaroni and Cheese

VEGETARIAN

One of my favorite things about the South is the sheer number of restaurants where you can order macaroni and cheese off the vegetable menu. I know eventually these "meat and three" restaurants will fade into memory, like so many of the things that make Southern food culture special, so I make an effort to savor them. In their honor I will continue to consider macaroni my vegetable portion of a meal, like the good Southerner that I am.

SERVES 4 TO 6

PREP TIME: 15 MINUTES

COOK TIME: 40 TO 45 MINUTES

1 pound dry macaroni

6 ounces fresh mozzarella cheese, cubed

1 tablespoon olive oil

1 cup whole milk

1 cup heavy cream

2 garlic cloves, minced

4 tablespoons salted butter

2 tablespoons all-purpose flour

1 cup shredded Swiss cheese

Juice of 1 lemon

1 teaspoon sea salt, plus more for seasoning

1 teaspoon cayenne

1 cup shredded Parmesan cheese

1. Preheat the oven to 350°F.

2. In a medium pot, cook the macaroni according to the package directi Drain the pasta and return it to the pot. Add the mozzarella and olive the pot and stir well.

3. In a small saucepan, scald the milk, cream, and garlic. Remove from heat and set aside.

4. Melt the butter in your skillet over medium heat. Slowly whisk the flou the butter, continuing to whisk for 1 to 2 minutes until it begins to thic and smooth out. Pour the milk mixture in, a little at a time, and whisk quickly to prevent clumping.

5. Add the Swiss cheese to the sauce, whisking constantly until the che melts. Remove the pan from the heat and add the lemon juice and s

6. Stir the pasta into the cheese sauce, mixing well to coat all the maca Sprinkle with the cayenne and salt. Top with the Parmesan cheese.

7. Bake for 35 to 40 minutes, until browned and bubbling.

Substitution tip: If you're a fan of mac and cheese with a crumb top, mix 1 cup of bread crumbs, ½ teaspoon of sea salt, and 4 tablespoons of melted butter in with the Parmesan before sprinkling it on top.

Black Bean Burger

VEGETARIAN → QUICK AND EASY → ONE-SKILLET MEAL

Homemade black bean burgers are superior in every way to those you find in the frozen foods section of a grocery store. They are thick, hearty, juicy, and full of flavor. I love them packed with spice and topped with all my favorite burger toppings.

SERVES 4

PREP TIME: 15 MINUTES

COOK TIME: 15 MINUTES

FOR THE PATTIES

1 small white onion, chopped

4 garlic cloves, halved

2 (15-ounce) cans black beans, drained, divided

1 teaspoon ground cumin

1 tablespoon Worcestershire sauce

Hot sauce

½ cup crumbled feta

1 teaspoon chipotle powder

½ teaspoon cayenne

1 egg

1 cup all-purpose flour

½ cup bread crumbs

1 tablespoon butter

2 tablespoons olive oil

FOR THE BURGERS

4 slices provolone cheese

4 hamburger buns

1 tablespoon butter

2 tablespoons mayonnaise

Lettuce

Tomato, thickly sliced

¼ red onion, thinly sliced

1. In a food processor, combine the onion, garlic, and half the black bea Blend until smooth.

2. In a large bowl, mix the black bean mixture with the remaining black beans, cumin, Worcestershire, a few shakes of hot sauce, feta, chipo powder, cayenne, egg, flour, and bread crumbs. Form the mixture int patties.

3. In your skillet, heat the oil over medium-high heat.

4. When the oil is hot, put the patties in the skillet. Cook for 5 minutes, the butter to the pan, and flip. Top each burger with a piece of chees Cook for an additional 5 minutes until cooked through and crisp. Tran to a plate in the microwave to keep warm.

5. While the burgers are cooking, spread the butter on the hamburger b Place them butter-side down on the skillet and toast for 1 to 2 minute

6. Spread the mayonnaise on the buns and layer a burger patty, lettuce tomato, and onion. Serve hot.

> Toddler tip: My son is not quite ready for the structure of a sandwich, so I offer him the burger with no bun. I simply halve the size of each patty and serve them with dipping sauce.

Tempeh Taco Skillet

VEGETARIAN → QUICK AND EASY → ONE-SKILLET MEAL

My son is a big fan of tempeh, something we started offering when he was a baby as a way to introduce different spices, and something that is an easy vegetarian winner in our house. This taco skillet combines spiced and crumbled tempeh with an all-star team of beans, rice, cheese, and fresh vegetables. It's a home run!

SERVES 4
PREP TIME: 10 MINUTES
COOK TIME: 15 MINUTES

8 ounces tempeh, crumbled

1 tablespoon tomato paste

3 garlic cloves, minced

½ teaspoon chipotle powder

½ teaspoon cayenne

1 teaspoon ground cumin

1 teaspoon chili powder

½ teaspoon sea salt

2 tablespoons olive oil

1 white onion, chopped

1 (15-ounce) can black beans, drained

1 cup white rice, cooked

1 cup shredded cheddar cheese

12 cherry tomatoes, halved

1 avocado, peeled, pitted, and sliced

1 cup cilantro, minced

Juice of 1 lime

Pinch sea salt

Hot sauce, for serving

1. In a medium bowl, mix the tempeh, tomato paste, garlic, chipotle, ca cumin, chili powder, and salt. Mix well.

2. In your skillet, heat the olive oil over medium heat. Add the onion to t skillet and cook for 3 to 4 minutes, until it starts to become transluce Add in the tempeh mixture.

3. Cook until the tempeh begins to brown, about 5 minutes. Stir in the b beans and white rice. Stir well to combine and cook for an additional minutes. When the rice and beans have warmed through and are ho enough to eat, stir in the cheese. Give the cheese a minute to melt a remove from the heat.

4. Top with the cherry tomatoes, avocado, and cilantro. Squeeze the lim sprinkle salt on top, then serve with a bottle of hot sauce.

Ingredient tip: For added depth of flavor, allow the tempeh to sit in the spices overnight in the refrigerator.

Black Bean and Avocado Tostadas

VEGETARIAN → QUICK AND EASY

I wrote this recipe, at 4 months pregnant, in the morning. And then I thought about it all day long. Finally, for dinner, I got to eat this tostada. It hit every note, one of the more wonderful pregnancy craving-to-fruition experiences, all tangy salsa and soft avocado. It was everything I wanted from the moment I thought about it, and it didn't disappoint.

SERVES 4
PREP TIME: 10 MINUTES
COOK TIME: 10 MINUTES

2 (15-ounce) cans black beans, drained but reserving ¼ cup liquid

1 teaspoon ground cumin

½ teaspoon paprika

¼ teaspoon red pepper flakes

1 teaspoon sea salt, divided

12 cherry tomatoes, halved

½ red onion, minced

Juice of 2 limes

½ cup fresh cilantro, minced

2 garlic cloves, minced

½ cup vegetable oil, for frying

4 corn tortillas

½ cup cotija cheese

1 cup shredded romaine lettuce (or your favorite salad green)

2 avocados, peeled, pitted, and sliced

1. In a saucepan over medium heat, combine the black beans, reserve liquid, cumin, paprika, red pepper flakes, and ½ teaspoon of salt. Co stirring frequently, until warmed through.

2. Reduce the heat to low, and simmer while stirring occasionally.

3. In a medium mixing bowl, combine the tomatoes, onion, lime juice, cilantro, garlic, and a pinch of salt. Stir well to combine and set aside

4. In your skillet, heat the vegetable oil over medium-high heat to 375°F

5. One at a time, fry the tortillas until they are crisp and golden brown, 4 60 seconds on each side. Transfer to a rack, sprinkle with salt, and a to cool.

6. Use a fork to gently mash the black beans and remove them from th

7. Plate each tortilla and top with a layer of black beans, cojita, lettuce, avocado, and salsa. Serve immediately.

Menu-planning tip: Try this with the Spicy Black Beans with Cotija.

Spinach and Ricotta Stuffed Shells

VEGETARIAN

The best thing about stuffed shells is the pasta-to-cheese ratio. Heavy cheese is how I want every ratio involving cheese to play out. Ricotta, Parmesan, and mozzarella come together to meet with the tangy tomato sauce and salty spinach. Plus, the cast-iron skillet creates nice crispy edges. It's a dream of a dinner.

SERVES 6 TO 8

PREP TIME: 39 MINUTES

COOK TIME: 1 HOUR 25 MINUTES

8 ounces large pasta shells

2 tablespoons olive oil

1 white onion, chopped

4 garlic cloves, minced

1 (6-ounce) can tomato paste

1 (28-ounce) can crushed tomatoes

¼ teaspoon red pepper flakes

1 teaspoon salt, divided

2 cups fresh spinach

2 cups ricotta cheese

1 egg

1 cup grated low-moisture mozzarella, divided

1 cup grated Parmesan cheese, divided

1 tablespoon dried oregano, divided

½ teaspoon freshly ground black pepper, divided

Handful fresh parsley, finely chopped

1. Parboil the pasta for ½ the recommended time on the box, so it is al Strain and set aside.

2. Heat the oven to 375°F.

3. In your skillet, heat 1 tablespoon of olive oil over medium heat. Add t onion and garlic and cook for 3 to 5 minutes, stirring frequently, until onions become translucent.

4. Add the tomato paste, stirring well to incorporate all the onions. Sme paste around the skillet to brown, then add the crushed tomatoes an pepper flakes. Stir so the tomato paste and the crushed tomatoes ful incorporate, then add ¼ teaspoon of salt and reduce the heat to a si Simmer for 20 to 25 minutes.

5. Remove the pan from the heat and transfer the sauce to a bowl.

6. Add the remaining tablespoon of olive oil to the skillet over medium h and quickly sauté the spinach. Cook for 2 to 3 minutes, stirring frequ until wilted.

7. In a small bowl, whisk together the ricotta, egg, ½ cup of mozzarella, cup of Parmesan, ½ tablespoon of oregano, ½ teaspoon of salt, and teaspoon of black pepper. Fold in the spinach.

8. Add half the tomato sauce to the skillet.

9. One at a time, stuff the shells with the ricotta mixture and nestle into skillet. Top with the remaining sauce, Parmesan, mozzarella, oregan and pepper.

10. Cover tightly with aluminum foil and bake for 40 minutes. Remove th and bake uncovered for an additional 10 minutes to brown the chees

11. Top with parsley and serve hot.

> Substitution tip: If large shells are hard to find, manicotti works just as well!

Sesame Cauliflower

VEGETARIAN → QUICK AND EASY

When I was diagnosed with celiac disease in 2015, a lot of my favorite restaurant foods were no longer an option. Even more disappointing, Chinese takeout was completely off the table. Between the fried options (clearly the best) and all the soy sauce, it all became out of reach—which is to say, it all became make-at-home! This sesame cauliflower hits all the notes of my favorite takeout orders: crispy, saucy, savory, and delicious.

SERVES 4

PREP TIME: 20 MINUTES

COOK TIME: 20 MINUTES

FOR THE CAULIFLOWER

½ cup vegetable oil

1 egg

¼ cup cornstarch

1 tablespoon garlic powder

1 tablespoon sesame oil

1 tablespoon soy sauce

1 head cauliflower, cut into florets

FOR THE SAUCE

1 tablespoon sesame oil

1" fresh ginger, peeled and finely chopped

3 garlic cloves, minced

¼ cup soy sauce

¼ cup honey

1 tablespoon rice vinegar

1 teaspoon sriracha

¼ cup water

½ tablespoon cornstarch

TO SERVE

4 cups cooked rice

1 tablespoon sesame seeds

Handful scallions, chopped

1. Heat the oven to 200°F. Place a baking sheet inside it to warm.

2. In your skillet, heat the vegetable oil over medium-high heat to 375°F

3. Whisk together the egg, cornstarch, garlic powder, sesame oil, and s sauce. Dip the cauliflower florets in the batter one at a time, then dro them into the hot oil.

4. Fry for 3 to 4 minutes per side, until crispy and browned. Transfer to baking sheet in the oven once they are done. Repeat with the remain cauliflower.

5. In a medium bowl, whisk together all the ingredients for the sauce un fully combined, then set aside.

6. In a saucepan over medium heat, warm the sauce. When it is simme add the cauliflower to the sauce, stirring to coat. Cook for 3 to 4 minu until the sauce is thickened.

7. Plate a cup of rice and top with cauliflower. Sprinkle with sesame see and scallions to serve.

> Substitution tip: Make this a full cauliflower experience by swapping rice for riced cauliflower.

Nashville Hot Chicken

CHAPTER 6: Seafood and Poultry

Whole Roast Chicken
Broiled Skillet Salmon
Chili Garlic Shrimp
Chicken Thighs over Root Vegetables
Crab Cakes
Chicken Piccata
Nashville Hot Chicken
Seared Scallops
Chicken and Broccoli Stir-Fry
Lemon Skillet Chicken
Skillet Paella
Sesame Chicken
Tuscan Chicken
Blackened Grouper
Chipotle Chicken Tacos

Whole Roast Chicken

This whole roasted chicken is for garlic lovers. And butter lovers. And crispy chicken skin lovers. This recipe calls for inserting the garlic cloves directly into the chicken before roasting, guaranteeing that the chicken is full of garlicky flavor. The bird also gets a buttery rub before hitting the oven, making the skin crispy to perfection.

SERVES 4 TO 6

PREP TIME: 10 MINUTES

INACTIVE TIME: 1 HOUR

COOK TIME: 1 HOUR

1 whole chicken

4 tablespoons salted butter, room temperature

10 garlic cloves

1 tablespoon sea salt

2 tablespoons olive oil, divided

1 tablespoon dried oregano

1 tablespoon minced fresh rosemary

1. Before you're planning to cook your chicken, take it out of the refrige Remove the innards, pat it dry, and let the chicken warm to room temperature for an hour. Tie the legs together to promote even roasti

2. Heat the oven to 475°F.

3. Rub the chicken with the butter, working it all over the skin and into t folds. Cut 10 slits, about 1" deep, throughout the chicken breasts an Stuff a garlic clove into each slit. Sprinkle with salt.

4. Coat your skillet with 1 tablespoon of olive oil and place the chicken i Drizzle with the remaining olive oil and top with the oregano and rose

5. Place the skillet in the oven and cook for 20 minutes, then drop the temperature to 400°F. Cook for an additional 40 minutes.

6. Remove the skillet from the oven and let the chicken rest for 10 minu before serving.

Menu-planning tip: Roast this chicken over root vegetables by following the Roasted Root Vegetables recipe.

Broiled Skillet Salmon

ONE-SKILLET MEAL

Salmon was a fish that I reluctantly came to as an adult. I grew up eating the sorts of mild white fish you can catch and prepare in the warm waters of the Gulf Stream or off the shore of North Carolina. Lox was my introduction to salmon, but I've come to love it in almost every form I've tried. With a slightly stronger flavor than grouper or flounder, salmon shines when it has the right combination of spice and acid supporting it.

SERVES 2
PREP TIME: 5 MINUTES
INACTIVE TIME: 1 HOUR
COOK TIME: 10 MINUTES

1 tablespoon olive oil

½ teaspoon sea salt

1 teaspoon smoked paprika

2 garlic cloves, minced

½ teaspoon red pepper flakes

½ teaspoon freshly ground black pepper

1 teaspoon fresh thyme, minced

1 teaspoon fresh oregano, minced

2 (4-ounce) salmon fillets

2 lemons, 1 juiced and 1 sliced

1. In a large, wide bowl, mix together the olive oil, salt, paprika, garlic, r pepper flakes, black pepper, thyme, and oregano. Nestle the salmon the marinade, skin-side up. Cover and chill for 1 hour.

2. Move the oven rack into a position 6" from the top and turn the broile high. Put your skillet in the oven and allow it to get hot, about 5 minu

3. Remove the skillet from the oven and place the salmon inside, skin-s down. Top with the lemon juice and return to the oven.

4. Broil for 5 minutes, then remove from the oven and arrange the lemo slices on top. Broil for an additional 3 to 4 minutes, until the salmon i cooked through and browned.

5. Serve immediately.

Ingredient tip: The longer the salmon rests in the marinade, the more delicious it will taste! Try marinating it overnight.

Chili Garlic Shrimp

QUICK AND EASY

One of my favorite food television moments of the past few years was watching the pure joy with which Samin Nosrat delighted in food on her Netflix series Salt, Fat, Acid, Heat. Her point that a delicious dish includes each of these components struck home, and I think that this shrimp is a wonderful example of these four elements working together in harmony.

SERVES 4
PREP TIME: 15 MINUTES
COOK TIME: 5 MINUTES

½ teaspoon salt

2 tablespoons chili garlic paste

3 garlic cloves, minced

1 tablespoon fish sauce

1 tablespoon soy sauce

1 pound large shrimp, peeled and deveined

1 tablespoon vegetable oil

2 tablespoons butter

Juice of ½ lime

Handful fresh cilantro, minced

1. In a medium bowl, mix together the salt, garlic paste, garlic, fish sau and soy sauce. Add the shrimp and stir well to coat.

2. In your skillet, heat the oil and butter over medium-high heat.

3. Add the shrimp and sauce, scraping every last bit from the bowl.

4. Cook for 4 to 5 minutes, stirring frequently, until the shrimp are pink a way through.

5. Remove from the heat and transfer to a serving dish. Top with the lim juice and cilantro, stir to coat, and serve.

> Menu-planning tip: To make this a meal, serve it on a bed of coconut rice. I whip it up quickly in an Instant Pot using 2 parts rice to 1 part water and 1 part coconut milk.

Chicken Thighs over Root Vegetables

ONE-SKILLET MEAL

Thighs are the unsung hero of chicken meat, the cut that doesn't get nearly the attention it deserves. Chicken thighs are full of flavor and can handle high temperatures without drying out, making them perfect for roasting and frying.

SERVES 4

PREP TIME: 20 MINUTES

COOK TIME: 35 TO 40 MINUTES

1 sweet potato, peeled and cubed

4 red potatoes, quartered

1 large carrot, peeled and cut into ½" rounds

4 shallots, quartered

5 garlic cloves, peeled

1 tablespoon olive oil

1 teaspoon sea salt, divided

4 bone-in, skin-on chicken thighs

2 tablespoons salted butter

2 tablespoons minced fresh rosemary

1 tablespoon minced fresh oregano

1 tablespoon minced fresh thyme

½ teaspoon freshly ground black pepper

1. Heat the oven to 475°F.

2. In your skillet, combine the sweet potato, red potatoes, carrot, shallo and garlic with the olive oil and ½ tablespoon of salt. Stir well to coat

3. Rub each chicken thigh with butter, then nestle them into the bed of vegetables. Top with the rosemary, oregano, thyme, remaining salt, a pepper.

4. Roast for 35 to 40 minutes, until the chicken temperature reaches 16

5. Toss the vegetables well before serving.

> Skill-building tip: If you don't have a meat thermometer, you can tell chicken is cooked when the internal juices run clear, not pink.

Crab Cakes

QUICK AND EASY → ONE-SKILLET MEAL

I had the good fortune of calling Baltimore home for a number of years, and one of my biggest takeaways was Marylanders' appreciation for crab. It's not that North Carolinians don't know their way around a crab; it's simply that nobody reveres the blue crab like Maryland folks do. During my years in Baltimore, I learned how to pick and cook them, how to season them, and how to achieve the perfect meat-to-filler ratio for a delicious crab cake. I've long since returned to my home state, but I'll always make crabs the Maryland way.

SERVES 4 TO 6

PREP TIME: 5 MINUTES

COOK TIME: 10 MINUTES

¼ cup vegetable oil

1 pound lump crab meat

1 egg

Juice of 1 lemon

1 tablespoon fresh parsley, minced

1 tablespoon fresh thyme, minced

2 tablespoons bread crumbs

¼ teaspoon sea salt

½ tablespoon Old Bay seasoning

Lemon wedges, for serving

1. In your skillet, heat the oil over medium-high heat to 375°F.

2. In a large mixing bowl, combine the crab meat, egg, lemon juice, par thyme, bread crumbs, salt, and Old Bay.

3. Stir well to combine, making sure the egg and bread crumbs are eve distributed.

4. Use your hands to form patties, each about 2" in diameter.

5. Fry each crab cake for 3 to 4 minutes, flip, and fry for an additional 3 minutes until they are crisp and golden brown all over.

6. Transfer to a rack to cool slightly before serving.

Menu-planning tip: I like to make a simple horseradish sauce to serve with my crab cakes. Whisk together ½ cup of mayonnaise, the juice of 1 lemon, 1 tablespoon of horseradish, and 1 tablespoon of minced fresh parsley.

Chicken Piccata

QUICK AND EASY

Growing up, my favorite food was lemon chicken (see the Lemon Skillet Chicken recipe), and although I still adore this dish, I also adore this slightly more sophisticated version. It has capers, butter, and a lovely wine sauce, which makes it irresistible.

SERVES 2

PREP TIME: 5 MINUTES

COOK TIME: 25 MINUTES

6 tablespoons salted butter, divided

4 tablespoons olive oil, divided

1 cup all-purpose flour

1 teaspoon sea salt, plus a pinch to season

½ teaspoon pepper

2 boneless, skinless chicken breasts, cut evenly in half

½ cup dry white wine (or chicken stock)

2 lemons, 1 juiced and 1 sliced thinly for serving

¼ cup brined capers

2 tablespoons minced fresh parsley

1. Heat the oven to 225°F and place a baking sheet inside to warm.

2. In your skillet, melt 2 tablespoons of butter over medium-high heat. M 2 tablespoons of olive oil.

3. In a medium bowl, mix the flour, salt, and pepper. Dredge the chicke breasts in the flour mixture and transfer them to the pan, two pieces

time. Cook for 3 to 4 minutes, flip, and cook for another 3 to 4 minute

4. Transfer the chicken from the skillet to the baking sheet in the oven a repeat with the remaining chicken, adding another 2 tablespoons of and 2 tablespoons olive oil to the skillet.

5. Once all the chicken is cooked, add the remaining butter, wine, lemo juice, salt, and capers to the skillet. Whisk together to get all the drip from the chicken. Cook for 3 to 4 minutes to thicken.

6. Plate the chicken and top each piece with a lemon slice, sauce, and parsley.

Ingredient tip: I like to use a dry white wine such as sauvignon blanc for this recipe, then serve the piccata with a glass of the same.

Nashville Hot Chicken

There are many restaurants in Nashville (and now, many restaurants around the country) that boast a hot chicken recipe, but the bones of the dish remain the same: buttermilk fried chicken, typically skillet fried, coated with a sauce made up primarily of lard and cayenne. This recipe often uses the reserved oil from frying in lieu of lard, but feel free to take a more authentic approach and try your hand at a lard-based sauce! (And, yes, a 12" skillet is deep enough to easily fry chicken.)

SERVES 8

PREP TIME: 15 MINUTES

INACTIVE TIME: OVERNIGHT

COOK TIME: 30 MINUTES

FOR THE MARINADE

2 cups buttermilk

1 tablespoon red pepper flakes

1 tablespoon cayenne

1 tablespoon sea salt

1½ teaspoons garlic powder

8 to 10 mixed bone-in, skin-on chicken breasts and thighs

FOR THE BREADING

3 cups all-purpose flour, divided

1 tablespoon red pepper flakes, divided

1 tablespoon cayenne, divided

1½ teaspoons garlic powder, divided

1 tablespoon sea salt, divided

4 eggs

2 tablespoons apple cider vinegar

2 cups bread crumbs

¼ cup yellow, coarse, stone-ground grits

Peanut oil for frying

FOR THE SPICY OIL

2 tablespoons hot sauce

2 tablespoons brown sugar

1 tablespoon cayenne

½ tablespoon smoked paprika

½ tablespoon garlic powder

1 teaspoon sea salt

1. In a large bowl, mix the buttermilk, red pepper flakes, cayenne, salt, garlic powder.

2. Add the chicken and turn to coat. Cover and marinate overnight in th refrigerator.

3. Line up three small bowls on your counter. In the first bowl, mix 1½ c flour, 1½ teaspoons of red pepper flakes, 1½ teaspoons of cayenne, teaspoon of garlic powder, and 1½ teaspoons of salt. In the second b whisk together the eggs and vinegar. In the third bowl, whisk togethe bread crumbs, grits, and remaining flour, red pepper flakes, cayenne garlic powder, and salt.

4. In your skillet, heat 1 inch of peanut oil over high heat to 375°F.

5. Working with one piece at a time, dip the chicken into the flour mixtu then the egg mixture, and then the bread crumb mixture.

6. Add the chicken to the hot oil and fry the breasts/white meat for 4 to minutes per side and thighs/dark meat for 6 to 7 minutes per side. D discard the frying oil.

7. Transfer to a wire rack to cool slightly.

8. In a heat-proof bowl, mix together the hot sauce, brown sugar, cayen paprika, garlic powder, salt, and ½ cup of reserved oil. Whisk well. B each piece of chicken with the spicy oil on all sides to coat before se

Menu-planning tip: Serve with white bread and dill pickle slices for an authentic Nashville-style hot chicken experience.

Seared Scallops

QUICK AND EASY

Scallops, harvested from the bottom of the sea floor, are difficult to acquire and absolutely worth the effort. These tender mollusks require a watchful eye, as overcooking can make them rubbery. Cook them with care, season them with butter, salt, and lemon juice, and you'll have a dish that is out-of-this-world delicious.

SERVES 3 TO 6
PREP TIME: 5 MINUTES
COOK TIME: 5 MINUTES

3 tablespoons salted butter

2 garlic cloves, minced

1 dozen sea scallops, rinsed and patted dry

Juice of 1 lemon

½ teaspoon sea salt

1. In your skillet, melt the butter over medium-high heat. Add the garlic skillet and stir.

2. Add the scallops and cook for 2 minutes, flip, and cook for an additio minutes.

3. Top with fresh lemon juice and salt and serve.

> Ingredient tip: Planning to open a bottle of wine? Add a splash of dry white wine to the pan after you've flipped the scallops to deepen the flavor.

Chicken and Broccoli Stir-Fry

QUICK AND EASY

Stir-fry is an ideal weeknight dinner because it's fast to pull together. We throw some rice in the Instant Pot, quickly cook the chicken and vegetables, and voilà, dinner is served. Stir-fry also has the benefit of being best when the vegetables are only lightly cooked, which makes it both full of flavor and exceedingly easy.

SERVES 4
PREP TIME: 15 MINUTES
COOK TIME: 20 MINUTES

2 tablespoons sesame oil, divided

2 boneless, skinless chicken breasts, thinly sliced and cut into 2" strips

3 garlic cloves, minced

1 onion, diced

1" fresh ginger, peeled and minced

1 head broccoli, stemmed and cut into florets

2 large carrots, peeled and cut into strips

2 cups shiitake mushrooms

2 cups snow peas

1 head bok choy, coarsely chopped

⅓ cup soy sauce

Cooked rice, for serving

1. In your skillet, heat 1 tablespoon of sesame oil over medium-high he Add the chicken and cook for 6 to 8 minutes, stirring frequently. Whe chicken is browned, transfer it to a plate and set aside.

2. Add the remaining sesame oil to the skillet over medium-high heat. A the garlic, onion, and ginger and cook for 2 to 3 minutes, until the oni have browned. Add the broccoli, carrots, and mushrooms and cook f additional 2 minutes, stirring frequently. Add the snow peas and bok Toss to combine and cook for another 2 minutes, until the boy choy h wilted.

3. Return the chicken to the skillet and add the soy sauce. Stir to coat a cook for an additional 2 minutes.

4. Serve over a bed of cooked rice.

> Substitution tip: Stir-fry is a wonderful way to showcase your favorite vegetables. Feel free to add bell peppers, button mushrooms, green beans, baby corn, or asparagus.

Lemon Skillet Chicken

Lemon chicken was my favorite food growing up. My house wasn't big on chicken nuggets, and this was as close as I could get. Crispy breading, strong lemony flavor, and tender chicken is a combination I still love many years later.

SERVES 4

PREP TIME: 10 MINUTES

COOK TIME: 10 MINUTES

1 cup all-purpose flour

3 lemons, 1 thinly sliced and 2 juiced, reserving 1 tablespoon zest

1 teaspoon sea salt, plus a pinch

2 boneless, skin-on chicken breasts, cut evenly in half

1 tablespoon olive oil

1 tablespoon butter

2 garlic cloves, minced

1. In a small bowl, combine the flour, lemon zest, and 1 teaspoon salt. Dredge the chicken.

2. In your skillet, combine the olive oil, butter, and garlic over medium h Sauté for 2 to 3 minutes, until the garlic has browned.

3. Add the chicken to the skillet, searing for 3 to 4 minutes per side. Re the skillet from the heat.

4. Top the chicken with the lemon slices and drizzle the lemon juice ove chicken. Sprinkle with salt and serve.

> Ingredient tip: For a stronger lemon flavor, marinate the chicken overnight with the juice of 1 lemon and a drizzle of olive oil.

Skillet Paella

ONE-SKILLET MEAL

My friend Aaron makes the most wonderful paella. It is beautiful and full of spicy chorizo and plump shrimp. He makes it for birthdays, parties, and even once for our baby shower. He's the only paella expert I know. So when I was developing this recipe, I knew I needed his input. I'm happy to say it got his full approval—and even a few compliments!

SERVES 4
PREP TIME: 25 MINUTES
COOK TIME: 35 MINUTES

¼ cup olive oil

5 garlic cloves, minced

1 white onion, chopped

2 cups Arborio rice

8 ounces Spanish chorizo, cubed

½ cup dry white wine

2½ cups chicken broth

4 large tomatoes, chopped

2 boneless, skinless chicken breasts

½ tablespoon smoked paprika

1 teaspoon saffron threads

1 teaspoon sea salt

½ teaspoon pepper

1 pound shrimp, peeled and deveined (tails optional)

6 to 12 mussels (depending on size), scrubbed and debearded

1 cup frozen peas, thawed

Juice of 2 lemons

1 tablespoon chopped fresh parsley

1. In your skillet, heat the olive oil over medium heat. Sauté the garlic a onion for 2 to 3 minutes, stirring frequently.

2. Add the rice and chorizo and cook for 3 to 4 minutes, stirring to coat.

3. Stir in the wine, allow it to evaporate, and then stir in the broth and tomatoes.

4. Bring to a strong simmer and add the chicken, paprika, saffron, salt, pepper. Stir well to coat and then cover to allow the rice and chicken cook for 12 to 15 minutes.

5. Remove the lid and stir thoroughly. Add the shrimp, mussels, and pe and stir well. Return the lid and cook for an additional 10 to 12 minut

6. When the shrimp is cooked through, the mussels are open, and the r soft, remove from the heat. Top with lemon juice and fresh parsley a serve.

> Ingredient tip: Aaron says he generally uses chicken thighs over chicken breasts, which can yield more overall fat but also moister meat. Try both and see what you prefer!

Sesame Chicken

QUICK AND EASY

Sesame chicken is a favorite of mine, one of the Chinese takeout options that I can't resist. The thick, flavorful sauce and the crisp, moist chicken is a delightful combination. This version has all the notes of takeout while being surprisingly easy to put together at home.

SERVES 4

PREP TIME: 10 MINUTES

COOK TIME: 10 MINUTES

FOR THE CHICKEN

½ cup vegetable oil

2 eggs

½ cup cornstarch

2 tablespoons garlic powder

2 tablespoons sesame oil

2 tablespoons soy sauce

4 chicken breasts, cubed

FOR THE SAUCE

2 tablespoons sesame oil

1" fresh ginger, peeled and finely chopped

4 garlic cloves, minced

½ cup soy sauce

⅓ cup honey

1 tablespoon rice vinegar

1 teaspoon sriracha

¼ cup water

½ tablespoon cornstarch

FOR SERVING

4 cups cooked rice

1 tablespoon sesame seeds

Handful scallions, chopped

1. Heat the oven to 200°F and place a baking sheet inside to warm.

2. In your skillet, heat the vegetable oil over medium-high heat to 375°F

3. Whisk together the eggs, cornstarch, garlic powder, sesame oil, and sauce. Dip the chicken pieces in the batter one at a time, then drop t into the hot oil.

4. Fry for 3 to 4 minutes per side, until crispy and browned. Transfer to baking sheet in the oven. Repeat with the remaining chicken.

5. In a medium bowl, whisk together all the ingredients for the sauce un fully combined, then set aside.

6. In a saucepan over medium heat, warm the sauce. When it is simme add the chicken, stirring to coat. Cook for 3 to 4 minutes, until the sa thickened.

7. Plate the rice and top with the chicken. Sprinkle with sesame seeds scallions to serve.

Menu-planning tip: I love to add steamed broccoli to the meal, giving it a good toss with the chicken before serving over rice.

Tuscan Chicken

QUICK AND EASY

This indulgent chicken dish is a family favorite and a true treat. The sweetness of the tomatoes pairs nicely with the creamy sauce, and the dish is rounded out by a good amount of fresh spinach.

SERVES 4

PREP TIME: 5 MINUTES

COOK TIME: 20 MINUTES

1 tablespoon olive oil

4 boneless, skinless chicken breasts

½ teaspoon sea salt

¼ teaspoon freshly ground black pepper

3 tablespoons salted butter

4 garlic cloves, minced

2 shallots, sliced

12 cherry tomatoes, halved

4 cups fresh spinach

¼ cup grated Parmesan cheese

½ cup heavy cream

Cooked rice, for serving

Juice of 1 lemon

1. In your skillet, heat the olive oil over medium heat.

2. Add the chicken and season with the salt and pepper. Cook for 6 to 8 minutes per side, until the chicken has browned and reached an inte

temperature of 160°F. Remove from the pan and set aside.

3. Add the butter, garlic, and shallots to the skillet. Cook for 2 to 3 minu until the shallots begin to soften. Add the tomatoes and spinach. Coo an additional 2 to 3 minutes, tossing well to coat the spinach.

4. Add the Parmesan and heavy cream to the pan and stir. Return the chicken to the pan and turn twice to coat it in the sauce. Cook an additional 2 to 3 minutes.

5. Serve on a bed of rice, dividing the sauce between four portions. Top lemon juice.

Skill-building tip: Slice the chicken into strips before returning it to the sauce to ensure that every piece is well sauced!

Blackened Grouper

QUICK AND EASY

Grouper is a plentiful fish off the coast of North Carolina, and a favorite in our kitchen. My father was a diver and a spear fisher and frequently supplied us with fresh grouper. We love it fried, breaded in sandwiches, and blackened with a spicy rub.

SERVES 4
PREP TIME: 10 MINUTES
COOK TIME: 10 MINUTES

1 teaspoon dried oregano

1 teaspoon freshly ground black pepper

1 teaspoon sea salt

½ teaspoon cayenne

¼ teaspoon red pepper flakes

¼ teaspoon ground cumin

1 teaspoon smoked paprika

4 (4-ounce) grouper fillets, cleaned and patted dry

4 tablespoons salted butter, melted

Juice of 1 lemon

1. In a small bowl, stir together the oregano, pepper, salt, cayenne, red pepper flakes, cumin, and paprika. Set aside.

2. Heat your dry skillet over medium-high heat.

3. Brush each fish fillet on both sides with melted butter and carefully c both sides with the spice mixture.

4. Add the fillets to the hot skillet and cook 2 to 3 minutes per side, until blackened and cooked through.

5. Drizzle the lemon juice over the fish and serve.

Substitution tip: For a spicier kick, substitute chipotle powder for the smoked paprika.

Chipotle Chicken Tacos

QUICK AND EASY → ONE-SKILLET MEAL

Tacos are a family favorite, particularly because my son loves any meal that involves assembling his own dish. There's huge appeal to anything he can pinch and sprinkle—especially cheese!

SERVES 4
PREP TIME: 10 MINUTES
COOK TIME: 10 MINUTES

FOR THE CHICKEN

2 chicken breasts, cubed

1 tablespoon olive oil, divided

1 teaspoon chipotle powder

½ teaspoon garlic powder

¼ teaspoon ground cumin

¼ teaspoon cayenne

¼ teaspoon sea salt

Juice of 1 lime

FOR THE TACOS

8 corn tortillas

1 cup pico de gallo

1 cup shredded pepper Jack cheese

1 cup shredded lettuce

1 lime, cut into wedges, for serving

½ cup sour cream, for serving

Hot sauce, for serving

1. In a small bowl, toss the chicken with ½ tablespoon of olive oil, chipo garlic, cumin, cayenne, and salt.

2. In your skillet, heat the remaining olive oil over medium-high heat.

3. Add the chicken and cook for 5 to 6 minutes. When the chicken com away freely from the skillet, flip. Cook for an additional 4 to 5 minutes

4. Squeeze the lime juice over the chicken and toss well to coat. Remo from the heat.

5. Assemble the tacos by layering a tortilla with chicken, pico de gallo, cheese, and lettuce. Serve with a lime wedge, sour cream, and hot s on the side.

> **Ingredient tip:** Corn tortillas truly shine when they're warm. Place the tortillas on a plate and cover with a damp towel. Microwave for 20 to 25 seconds until warmed through.

Sriracha and Ginger Hamburgers

CHAPTER 7: Meat

Shepherd's Pie
Cubano Sandwich
Perfect Cast-Iron Steak
Sriracha and Ginger Hamburgers
Cheeseburger Tacos
Marinated Steak Fajitas
Sloppy Joes
Honey Mustard Pork Chops
Fried Bologna Sandwiches
Beef and Broccoli
Sausage, Peppers, and Rice
Pasta Carbonara
Roast Beef Tenderloin
Bacon and Onion Meatloaf
Beef Stew Skillet Pie

Shepherd's Pie

When it's cold, rainy, and dreary, shepherd's pie is precisely the meal I want to eat. It's hearty, packed full of flavor, and oh so comforting. (I mean, it has mashed potatoes, so what is not to love?) Also, it has the added benefits of usually producing leftovers and being one of those perfect meals that tastes even better the next day. And that's great, because dreary days usually come in pairs.

SERVES 4 TO 6

PREP TIME: 15 MINUTES

COOK TIME: 1 HOUR 10 MINUTES

FOR THE MASHED POTATOES

3 russet potatoes, peeled and quartered

1 stick salted butter

½ cup mayonnaise

1 teaspoon sea salt

1 teaspoon freshly ground black pepper

FOR THE FILLING

2 tablespoons olive oil, divided

2 shallots, thinly sliced

4 garlic cloves, minced, divided

1 pound ground beef, 85% lean

1 tablespoon herbes de Provence

1 teaspoon ground cumin

¼ teaspoon red pepper flakes

¼ teaspoon sea salt

2 cups peas

2 large carrots, peeled and cubed

1. Bring a large pot of salted water to boil. Add the potatoes and cook u tender, 13 to 15 minutes.

2. In the bowl of a stand mixer, or a large bowl with a hand mixer, comb the cooked potatoes, butter, mayonnaise, salt, and pepper. Mix on m speed until creamy. Adjust the seasoning to taste. Set aside.

3. In your skillet, heat 1 tablespoon of olive oil over medium heat. Add t shallots and half the garlic, cooking for 3 to 4 minutes, until they begi soften. Add the ground beef, herbes de Provence, cumin, red peppe flakes, and salt.

4. Cook for 10 to 12 minutes, stirring frequently, until the beef is cooked through.

5. Transfer the beef to a medium bowl and set aside.

6. Heat the oven to 400°F.

7. Heat the remaining olive oil in the skillet and sauté the remaining gar Add the peas and carrots and cook for 3 to 4 minutes. Remove from heat and transfer the vegetables to a small bowl.

8. Return the beef to the skillet and top with the peas and carrots. Add mashed potatoes, spreading evenly over the beef and vegetables, m sure that the potatoes "kiss" the side of the skillet.

9. Bake for 30 minutes, until browned on top and bubbling.

Substitution tip: Technically speaking, this is a cottage pie. A true shepherd's pie would have ground lamb instead of beef. Make the swap and try an authentic shepherd's pie!

Cubano Sandwich

QUICK AND EASY → ONE-SKILLET MEAL

When you're pregnant, it can sometimes feel like the list of foods you're allowed to eat is shorter than the list of foods you're not. In addition to big game fish, soft cheeses, wine coolers, and sprouts, you're also supposed to avoid deli meats. This is generally fine except for when I'm packing my son's lunch and all of a sudden I need a piece of ham. In comes the humble Cubano, a sandwich that is not only insanely good but also heats up enough in the middle to make it pregnancy safe, meaning that I can have my ham and eat it, too.

SERVES 2
PREP TIME: 5 MINUTES
COOK TIME: 10 MINUTES

2 tablespoons mayonnaise

2 tablespoons spicy brown mustard

4 slices thick-cut bread or bakery rolls

4 slices ham

1 cup pulled pork

4 slices Swiss cheese

8 dill pickle slices

2 tablespoons butter

1. In a small bowl, mix together the mayonnaise and mustard. Spread t mixture evenly on the 4 slices of bread.

2. Layer both bottom slices with ham, pulled pork, cheese, and pickles. with the remaining slices of bread.

3. In your skillet, melt the butter over medium-high heat. Cook the sandwiches for 2 to 3 minutes per side, just long enough to crisp the and melt the cheese.

4. Serve immediately.

> Substitution tip: If you don't live in a place where pulled pork is widely available, this also works well with roasted pork tenderloin slices.

Perfect Cast-Iron Steak

QUICK AND EASY

Absolutely nothing is better than a perfectly cooked steak. The key to steak success is the simple but crucial combination of a quality pan and a good cut of meat. Steak and the cast-iron skillet were made for each other. The heavy nonstick pan allows for a perfect sear and slight char, and with the help of some butter and garlic, it's heaven.

SERVES 2
PREP TIME: 5 MINUTES
COOK TIME: 15 MINUTES

1 pound beef strip steak, 1" thick, at room temperature

1 teaspoon sea salt

½ teaspoon freshly ground black pepper

3 tablespoons salted butter, divided

1 garlic clove, minced

1. Pat the steak dry and sprinkle each side with salt and pepper.

2. In your skillet, melt 2 tablespoons of butter over medium-high heat.

3. Add the garlic to the skillet. Cook for 1 minute, stirring frequently, unt begins to brown.

4. Add the steak. Cook for 5 minutes and flip. For a rare steak, cook 3 t more minutes, until the internal temperature reaches 135°F. For a m steak, cook 5 to 7 more minutes, until the internal temperature reach 140°F. For a medium-well steak, cook for 8 to 10 more minutes, until internal temperature reaches 150°F.

5. Transfer the steak to a plate and let it rest for 5 minutes.

6. Top with the remaining 1 tablespoon of butter and serve.

> Ingredient tip: I like strip steak because it's a high-quality cut that doesn't require much more than a bit of seasoning to be delicious. I choose organic, grass-fed options that have a good amount of marbling and are within my budget.

Sriracha and Ginger Hamburgers

QUICK AND EASY → ONE-SKILLET MEAL

My husband, Dan, makes the absolute best burgers. I am convinced that it's the combination of a well-seasoned patty, a buttered and toasted bun, and a healthy spread of mayonnaise. (We are firmly in the Duke's camp, although Hellman's is acceptable.) One of his favorite combinations is sriracha and ginger, which gives enough heat to keep it interesting without being overpowering.

SERVES 4
PREP TIME: 5 MINUTES
COOK TIME: 15 MINUTES

FOR THE PATTIES

1 pound ground beef, 85% lean

2 garlic cloves, minced

1 teaspoon ground ginger

2 tablespoons sriracha

½ teaspoon sea salt

1 tablespoon olive oil

4 slices provolone cheese

FOR THE BURGER

¼ cup mayonnaise

1 tablespoon sriracha

¼ teaspoon ground ginger

4 hamburger buns

½ red onion, thinly sliced

1 cup fresh greens (arugula, spinach, lettuce)

1. In a medium bowl, combine the ground beef, garlic, ginger, sriracha, salt. Mix well to distribute the seasoning.

2. Divide the mixture into four balls and form into patties.

3. In your skillet, heat the olive oil over medium-high heat.

4. Cook the patties for 5 to 7 minutes, flip, and put a slice of cheese on burger. Cook for an additional 5 to 7 minutes.

5. While the burgers are cooking, mix together the mayonnaise, srirach ginger in a small bowl. Spread evenly on the inside of each bun.

6. Layer the hamburger, red onions, and greens on each bun and serve

Ingredient tip: I prefer a toasted bun, so after I finish the burgers, I quickly wipe out the skillet, spread butter on the inside of each bun, and toast for 1 to 2 minutes until browned.

Cheeseburger Tacos

QUICK AND EASY → ONE-SKILLET MEAL

There is a restaurant in town that, for a while, had cheeseburger tacos on the "secret menu," much to the delight of my husband, Dan, because it blended his two favorite dishes. This is one of the more ridiculous (but still totally delicious) examples of fusion. The tortilla is loaded with seasoned ground beef, cheese, lettuce, pickles, tomato, and spicy mayonnaise. Now the secret's out.

SERVES 4

PREP TIME: 15 MINUTES

COOK TIME: 10 MINUTES

FOR THE MEAT

1 tablespoon olive oil

1 pound ground beef, 85% lean

1 teaspoon ground cumin

1 teaspoon smoked paprika

½ teaspoon sea salt

FOR THE SAUCE

½ cup mayonnaise

1 tablespoon sriracha

1 tablespoon spicy brown mustard

1 teaspoon apple cider vinegar or pickle juice

FOR ASSEMBLING

8 flour tortillas

1 cup shredded cheddar cheese

1 large tomato, diced

½ cup dill pickle slices

1 cup shredded lettuce

¼ cup red onion slices

1. In your skillet, heat the olive oil over medium heat.

2. Add the beef, cumin, paprika, and salt. Cook for 8 to 10 minutes, stir occasionally, until the beef has browned and cooked through.

3. While the beef is cooking, whisk together the mayonnaise, sriracha, mustard, and vinegar in a small bowl.

4. Layer a tortilla with beef, cheese, tomatoes, pickles, lettuce, and onio Drizzle each taco with the sauce and serve immediately.

Fun tip: Our favorite restaurant tacos come with a hard shell and a soft shell. The filling goes in the hard shell and then a layer of sauce is spread on the soft tortilla, which is wrapped around the hard shell.

Marinated Steak Fajitas

ONE-SKILLET MEAL

There are few dishes better suited to cast iron than fajitas. Cooked fast and at high heat, they show off the skillet's nonstick superpowers, and the heat retention makes this dish perfect for serving tableside, still sizzling in the skillet.

SERVES 4

PREP TIME: 10 MINUTES

INACTIVE TIME: 1 HOUR (OR OVERNIGHT)

COOK TIME: 10 MINUTES

FOR THE MARINATED STEAK

2 tablespoons olive oil

Juice of 2 limes

2 garlic cloves, minced

1 tablespoon chipotle powder

½ teaspoon cayenne

1 teaspoon ground cumin

Handful fresh cilantro, chopped

1 pound skirt steak, marinated

FOR THE FAJITAS

2 tablespoons olive oil, divided

1 large yellow onion, sliced

1 red bell pepper, cut into ½" strips

1 green bell pepper, cut into ½" strips

3 garlic cloves, minced

½ teaspoon sea salt

FOR SERVING

10 (6") corn tortillas

Sour cream

Cilantro

Lime wedges

1. In a wide, medium bowl, combine the olive oil, lime juice, garlic, chip cayenne, cumin, and cilantro. Add the steak to the bowl, turning onc coat.

2. Cover and chill for at least one hour, or overnight.

3. In your skillet, heat 1 tablespoon of olive oil over medium-high heat.

4. Pat the steak dry. Cook the steak for 2 to 3 minutes, flip, and cook fo 3 more minutes. Remove the steak from the heat and set aside.

5. Add the remaining olive oil to the skillet along with the onion, pepper garlic. Cook for 6 to 8 minutes, stirring frequently, until the onion beg brown. Remove from the heat.

6. Thinly slice the steak and return it to the pan. Season with salt, stir w and heat for an additional 2 to 3 minutes until sizzling.

7. Serve very hot with tortillas and sour cream, cilantro, and lime wedge the side.

> Substitution tip: If you can't find skirt steak, flank steak also works well for this recipe.

Sloppy Joes

QUICK AND EASY → ONE-SKILLET MEAL

Sloppy Joes were a childhood favorite of mine, one that I can still reach back into my mind and taste. Now that I'm a parent myself, I feel absolutely no rush to introduce my son, who has yet to fully master the structure of a sandwich, to the aptly named Sloppy Joe—but maybe on bath night?

SERVES 4
PREP TIME: 5 MINUTES
COOK TIME: 25 MINUTES

1 tablespoon salted butter

1 pound ground beef, 85% lean

½ yellow onion, diced

3 garlic cloves, minced

¾ cup ketchup

8 ounces crushed tomatoes

¼ teaspoon sea salt

2 tablespoons hot sauce

1 tablespoon Worcestershire sauce

½ tablespoon brown sugar

1 tablespoon spicy brown mustard

1 teaspoon smoked paprika

¼ teaspoon red pepper flakes

4 hamburger buns

1. In your skillet, melt the butter over medium-high heat. Add the groun to the pan and stir to break up.

2. Cook for 3 to 4 minutes until browned. Add the onion and garlic, stir, continue to cook.

3. In a medium bowl, whisk together the ketchup, tomatoes, salt, hot sa Worcestershire sauce, sugar, mustard, paprika, and red pepper flake

4. Add the tomato mixture to the skillet, stirring well to coat the beef.

5. Once the pan is bubbling, cover and reduce the heat, simmering for 15 minutes.

6. Remove the cover and stir. Season to taste.

7. Scoop a generous amount onto each bun and serve hot.

Menu-planning tip: Serve with a side of tortilla chips for cleaning up the delicious mess!

Honey Mustard Pork Chops

QUICK AND EASY

Where I live, dangerously close to the South Carolina border, you'll sometimes find barbecue with a mustard-based sauce. Now, I am incredibly picky about my barbecue and will only eat it with an Eastern North Carolina apple cider vinegar sauce. However, I find the mustard sauce to be lovely on other things, including pork chops. This version has a little extra sweetness, thanks to a drizzle of honey, and it's fantastic with these salty and skillet-seared chops.

SERVES 2
PREP TIME: 10 MINUTES
COOK TIME: 15 MINUTES

¼ cup Dijon mustard

1 tablespoon honey

½ tablespoon garlic powder

2 tablespoons apple cider vinegar

2 bone-in pork chops

½ teaspoon sea salt

½ teaspoon freshly ground black pepper

1 tablespoon olive oil

1. Heat the oven to 375°F.

2. In a small bowl, whisk together the mustard, honey, garlic powder, an vinegar. Set aside.

3. Pat the pork chops dry and season with salt and pepper on both side

4. In your skillet, heat the olive oil over medium-high heat. Add the pork chops and sear on both sides for 3 to 4 minutes.

5. Top with the sauce, flipping to coat both sides, and transfer the chop the oven. Cook for 10 to 12 minutes.

6. Serve immediately.

Substitution tip: For a tangier sauce, drop the honey and double the amount of apple cider vinegar.

Fried Bologna Sandwiches

QUICK AND EASY → ONE-SKILLET MEAL

Of all the silly advertisements that have stuck in my head over the years (looking at you, early aughts TV commercials), the Biscuitville proclamation that "fried bologna is back" is my favorite. It popped up somewhat regularly here in North Carolina, giving the impression that fried bologna had an arbitrary schedule and perhaps only went away so as to return and allow for promotion. Either way, I think about it all the time, and it always makes me want a fried bologna sandwich. So, essentially, brilliant advertising.

SERVES 2

PREP TIME: 5 MINUTES

COOK TIME: 10 MINUTES

2 tablespoons mayonnaise

1 tablespoon spicy brown mustard

4 slices bologna, with a slit cut from the middle to the end to prevent curling

4 slices bread (honestly, white bread is made for this)

2 tablespoons butter

1. In a small bowl, mix together the mayonnaise and mustard.

2. Heat your dry skillet over medium-high heat.

3. Cook the bologna for 2 to 3 minutes per side, until well browned. Re from the heat.

4. Spread an even amount of the mayonnaise mixture on each slice of Build your sandwiches with two slices of bread and two pieces of bol

5. Return the pan to the heat and melt the butter. Place the sandwiches the skillet and cook 2 to 3 minutes per side to toast.

6. Serve hot.

Menu-planning tip: For extra flavor and some crunch, try adding pickles and lettuce inside your fried bologna sandwich.

Beef and Broccoli

Beef and broccoli, with tender meat simmered in a flavorful sauce and broccoli cooked to perfection, is a family favorite. It is delicious served over rice or noodles, and it tastes even better the next day.

SERVES 4

PREP TIME: 10 MINUTES

INACTIVE TIME: 30 MINUTES

COOK TIME: 20 MINUTES

½ cup soy sauce

1 tablespoon sriracha or chili paste

Juice of 2 limes

1 tablespoon brown sugar

2 tablespoons cornstarch, divided

1 tablespoon minced fresh ginger

2 garlic cloves, minced

1 pound flank steak, thinly sliced

2 tablespoons vegetable oil

½ cup beef broth

1 head broccoli, cut into florets

1 tablespoon sesame seeds, for garnish

Cooked rice, for serving

1. In a medium bowl, combine the soy sauce, sriracha, lime juice, brow sugar, 1 tablespoon of cornstarch, ginger, and garlic. Divide the sauc half and marinate the steak in one portion of the liquid, turning well to Set the other half of the sauce aside.

2. Allow the beef to marinate in the sauce for 25 to 30 minutes.

3. In your skillet, heat the oil over medium-high heat. Add the beef and the marinade to the skillet. Cook for 3 to 4 minutes, flip, and cook for additional 3 to 4 minutes. Remove to a plate.

4. Add the remaining sauce to the skillet, along with the beef broth and remaining cornstarch.

5. Reduce the heat to medium and whisk well to distribute the cornstar Cook for 3 to 4 minutes, stirring frequently, until the sauce begins to thicken.

6. Add the broccoli. Stir to coat the broccoli, then cook until it's bright gr and tender, 4 to 5 minutes. Add the steak back to the pan and cook f additional 2 to 3 minutes.

7. Serve hot over rice. Garnish with sesame seeds.

Substitution tip: My dad loved to eat his beef and broccoli on a bed of chow mein. Boil the noodles, and once you've removed the beef and broccoli from the skillet, quickly stir-fry the noodles in the sauce, then combine and serve.

Sausage, Peppers, and Rice

QUICK AND EASY → ONE-SKILLET MEAL

Any variation of sausage and rice is a big hit in our house. Our son is deeply committed to any sausage dish, so we try to pepper it into our weekly dinners to keep on his good side. This dish, with a Cajun flair, is a favorite in the rotation.

SERVES 4
PREP TIME: 10 MINUTES
COOK TIME: 20 MINUTES

1 tablespoon olive oil

1 pound andouille sausage, cut into ¼" slices

1 green bell pepper, cut into strips

1 red bell pepper, cut into strips

1 large white onion, diced

3 garlic cloves, minced

1 tablespoon tomato paste

½ cup chicken broth

2 cups cooked rice

1 teaspoon Cajun seasoning

½ teaspoon sea salt

1. In your skillet, heat the olive oil over medium heat.

2. Brown the andouille in the skillet for 1 to 2 minutes per side, and set

3. Add the peppers, onion, and garlic to the skillet. Cook for 4 to 5 minu stirring frequently, until the peppers and onions have browned. Trans

a plate.

4. Add the tomato paste, broth, rice, Cajun seasoning, and salt to the s Stir well to coat the rice and return the sausage to the skillet. Cook fo 3 minutes, stirring frequently, then return the peppers and onions to t skillet. Cook for an additional 2 to 3 minutes, stirring frequently.

5. Season to taste and serve.

Substitution tip: For more heat, add ¼ teaspoon of cayenne.

Pasta Carbonara

QUICK AND EASY

Every year we throw a dinner party on the occasion of the winter solstice, a small gathering to mark the shortest day of the year and the return of the sun. Unintentionally, I've settled into a fixed menu for this dinner, mostly because there are a handful of classic favorites that immediately come to mind when I'm planning. Alongside a salad with a hot bacon dressing and a classic yule log cake, every year I make pasta carbonara. It's truly a crowd pleaser, something everyone wants seconds of, and it has the added benefit of coming together quickly—which is especially helpful when you're also making a rolled cake!

SERVES 4
PREP TIME: 5 MINUTES
COOK TIME: 15 MINUTES

2 large eggs

1 cup grated Parmesan cheese, plus more for serving

1 tablespoon olive oil

2 tablespoons butter

1 pound bacon, cut into 1" pieces

2 garlic cloves, minced

1 pound spaghetti

1 teaspoon sea salt

½ teaspoon freshly ground black pepper

⅓ cup coarsely chopped fresh parsley

1. In a mixing bowl, whisk together the eggs and Parmesan. Set aside. the oil and butter over medium-high heat. Add the bacon and cook fo

10 minutes, stirring occasionally, until cooked through and browned. the garlic to the pan.

2. While the meat is cooking, boil the pasta in salted water.

3. When the noodles are cooked, strain and reserve ¼ cup of the pasta water.

4. Remove the skillet from the heat and toss the noodles with the baco coating with the drippings. Add the egg mixture and reserved water, quickly to coat the noodles.

5. Plate and top with the salt, pepper, parsley, and fresh Parmesan.

Ingredient tip: I also love to add half a pound of spicy loose sausage to the bacon for an added layer of flavor.

Roast Beef Tenderloin

Roast beef is one of my favorite deli meats, and making it at home means that I get to enjoy it fresh from the oven and thinly sliced in the form of leftovers, which is the best of both worlds.

SERVES 8 TO 10

PREP TIME: 10 MINUTES

INACTIVE TIME: 1 HOUR

COOK TIME: 30 MINUTES

FOR THE ROAST BEEF

1 beef tenderloin, trimmed of fat

2 tablespoons salted butter, room temperature

3 garlic cloves, minced

1 teaspoon sea salt

1 teaspoon crushed black peppercorns

1 tablespoon minced fresh rosemary

1 tablespoon minced fresh thyme

2 tablespoons olive oil

FOR THE SAUCE

1 cup Greek yogurt

⅓ cup jarred horseradish

1 tablespoon spicy brown mustard

½ teaspoon sea salt

1 teaspoon apple cider vinegar

1 tablespoon minced chives

1 tablespoon mayonnaise

1. Take the beef out of the refrigerator 1 hour before cooking to allow it come to room temperature.

2. Heat the oven to 475°F.

3. In a small bowl, mix together the butter, garlic, salt, pepper, rosemar thyme.

4. Use twine to tie tight circles around the beef in 2" intervals to ensure cooking.

5. Rub the butter and herb mixture all over the beef. Place the prepared tenderloin in your skillet and drizzle with the olive oil.

6. Roast in the oven for 25 to 30 minutes, until the internal temperature 125°F.

7. While the beef is roasting, whisk together the yogurt, horseradish, mustard, salt, vinegar, chives, and mayonnaise in a small bowl.

8. Allow the beef to rest for 10 minutes before slicing. Then slice into 1" rounds and serve warm with the horseradish sauce.

> Menu-planning tip: When it comes to leftovers, I love to load thin slices of roast beef onto thick bread with a huge dollop of horseradish sauce, fresh arugula, and provolone cheese.

Bacon and Onion Meatloaf

Meatloaf is a meal that I forget about, sometimes for years, until it comes to mind one day and suddenly I need it. There's no thinking about meatloaf and moving on with your day; there is only thinking about meatloaf and then making meatloaf as quickly as possible so you can eat it. And what's not to love? It's easy, it makes plenty of leftovers, and it feeds a part of your soul you didn't realize was hungry.

SERVES 4 TO 6

PREP TIME: 10 MINUTES

COOK TIME: 1 HOUR

FOR THE MEATLOAF

2 pounds ground beef, 85% lean

1 cup bread crumbs

½ cup tomato paste

½ cup whole milk

4 garlic cloves, minced

2 eggs, lightly beaten

1 white onion, finely chopped

8 ounces bacon, cooked and crumbled, 2 tablespoons reserved

1 teaspoon sea salt

1 teaspoon garlic powder

1 teaspoon smoked paprika

1 teaspoon dry mustard

½ teaspoon cayenne

FOR THE SAUCE

½ cup apple cider vinegar

3 tablespoons packed brown sugar

½ cup tomato paste

1. Preheat the oven to 350°F.

2. In a large bowl, mix the ground beef, bread crumbs, tomato paste, m garlic, eggs, onion, bacon, salt, garlic powder, paprika, dry mustard, cayenne.

3. Press the meat mixture into your skillet.

4. In a small bowl, whisk together the apple cider vinegar, brown sugar, tomato paste. Brush half of the sauce evenly over the top of the mea

5. Bake for 1 hour.

6. Top with the remaining sauce and reserved bacon crumbles. Serve h

> **Menu-planning tip:** Meatloaf should always be served with mashed potatoes. Here's a quick recipe: In a mixer, combine 3 potatoes, peeled, cubed, and boiled until tender; ½ cup of mayonnaise; 2 tablespoons of butter; and salt and pepper to taste. Mix until smooth, then add the juice of ½ a lemon. Add more mayo if you prefer creamier mashed potatoes. (Yes, mayo.)

Beef Stew Skillet Pie

ONE-SKILLET MEAL

This past Christmas, I watched a BBC Christmas special (in the tub with a glass of wine) featuring former Great British Bake Off judge Mary Berry and the Duke and Duchess of Cambridge, which was an unbelievably lovely experience. It was comforting and entertaining and made me very much want a scone and a bowl of beef stew—but not at the same time! This beef stew is loosely based on Mary's but with more root vegetables and a pie crust on top.

SERVES 4 TO 6

PREP TIME: 20 MINUTES, PLUS 20 MINUTES TO CHILL

COOK TIME: 1 HOUR

FOR THE DOUGH

1¼ cups all-purpose flour

1 teaspoon paprika

¼ teaspoon salt

1½ sticks cold butter, cubed

2 to 4 tablespoons cold water

1 egg

FOR THE FILLING

1 tablespoon olive oil

1 pound stew beef, cubed

1 tablespoon salted butter

1 leek, thinly sliced

5 red potatoes, quartered

1 large carrot, cut into ½" rounds

1 onion, minced

4 garlic cloves, minced

1 teaspoon ground ginger

1 tablespoon Worcestershire sauce

2 tablespoons all-purpose flour

1 teaspoon sea salt

½ cup red wine

2 cups beef broth

1. In a large bowl, combine the flour, paprika, salt, and butter. Use your hands to cut the butter in, until the texture resembles cornmeal. Pour water, a little at a time, until a dough ball forms. Wrap the dough in pl wrap and chill for 20 to 30 minutes.

2. In your skillet, heat the oil over medium heat. Add the beef and brow all sides, 4 to 5 minutes, and then remove to a plate.

3. Add the butter to the hot skillet. Once it begins to melt, add the leek, potatoes, carrots, onion, and garlic. Cook for 4 to 5 minutes, stirring frequently, until tender and brown around the edges.

4. Stir in the ginger, Worcestershire sauce, flour, and salt. Stir to coat, t add the red wine. Add the beef broth to the pan and stir to combine. Reduce the heat and simmer for 10 to 15 minutes, stirring occasiona

5. Heat the oven to 400°F.

6. While the meat is simmering, roll out the dough onto a floured surfac Shape it into a 13" round.

7. Remove the skillet from the heat and stir the stew well to redistribute liquid. Place the pie dough on top, pressing it in around the edges of skillet. Cut 4 slits from the center toward the edges, about 3" in lengt

8. Whisk the egg in a small bowl, then brush over the top of the dough.

9. Bake the pie for 25 to 30 minutes, until the crust is golden brown. Se warm.

> Menu-planning tip: Mary Berry serves her beef stew with a horseradish sauce. The sauce here would be the perfect accompaniment!

Strawberry Skillet Cake

CHAPTER 8: Dessert

Chocolate Chip Bread Pudding with Whiskey Sauce
Chocolate Cake with Whipped Hazelnut Icing
Buttermilk Pound Cake with Blackberry Jam
Strawberry Skillet Cake
Monster Skillet Cookie
Churros
Apple Pie
Chocolate Pecan Pie
Berry Buckle
Vinegar Pie

Chocolate Chip Bread Pudding with Whiskey Sauce

VEGETARIAN

This bread pudding is pretty decadent. So decadent, in fact, that it usually makes an appearance in my family around the holidays, when all rules go out the window, and the more whipped cream, the better.

SERVES 4 TO 6

PREP TIME: 15 MINUTES

COOK TIME: 45 MINUTES

FOR THE PUDDING

¼ cup salted butter, for greasing

1 loaf French bread, preferably a day old, broken into 1" pieces

1 cup chocolate chips

5 eggs

2 cups whole milk

1 cup heavy cream

½ cup sugar

¼ teaspoon ground cinnamon

¼ teaspoon ground nutmeg

¼ teaspoon ground ginger

¼ teaspoon vanilla extract

FOR THE SAUCE

2 cups heavy cream

2 tablespoons salted butter

½ cup sugar

¾ cup whiskey

2 tablespoons cornstarch

FOR THE CREAM

1 cup heavy whipping cream

1 tablespoon sugar

1 teaspoon vanilla extract

1. Preheat the oven to 350°F.

2. Grease your skillet with the butter and evenly arrange the bread piec inside. Sprinkle with the chocolate chips.

3. In a large bowl, whisk the eggs, milk, heavy cream, sugar, cinnamon nutmeg, ginger, and vanilla. Pour over the top of the bread. Do not m

4. Bake for 45 minutes, remove from the oven, and cool, letting the fillin before serving.

5. While the pudding is in the oven, combine the cream, butter, and sug a saucepan over medium heat. Scald and reduce the heat to low.

6. Whisk together the whiskey and cornstarch and stir into the cream, s constantly until the sauce has thickened. Remove from the heat and aside.

7. In a stand mixer, or with a hand mixer, combine the whipping cream, and vanilla. Whip on high until soft peaks form. Chill.

8. When the bread pudding comes out of the oven, drizzle with the whi sauce and serve with whipped cream on the side.

Substitution tip: Some New Orleans–style whiskey bread puddings call for golden raisins in place of chocolate chips.

Chocolate Cake with Whipped Hazelnut Icing

VEGETARIAN

Since my first lick of Nutella in childhood, I have been deeply dedicated to the chocolate-hazelnut spread. I will hoard Ferrero Rocher chocolates during the holidays and cannot pass up hazelnut ganache on a dessert menu. It stands to reason that this cake, with its crispy edges and whipped hazelnut icing, would be a favorite of mine.

SERVES 6 TO 8
PREP TIME: 20 MINUTES
COOK TIME: 35 MINUTES

FOR THE CAKE

1 cup cocoa powder

2½ cups all-purpose flour

2 teaspoons baking powder

1 teaspoon baking soda

1 teaspoon salt

½ stick butter, room temperature

1½ cups granulated sugar

3 eggs

¼ cup vegetable oil

2 teaspoons vanilla extract

1 cup buttermilk

1 tablespoon butter, for greasing

FOR THE ICING

1 stick butter, room temperature

¾ cup hazelnut spread

3 cups powdered sugar

1 teaspoon vanilla extract

¼ cup heavy cream

1. Heat the oven to 350°F.

2. In a large bowl, sift together the cocoa, flour, baking powder, baking and salt.

3. In the bowl of a stand mixer, or in a large bowl with a hand mixer, cre the butter and sugar.

4. In a small bowl, combine the eggs, oil, vanilla, and buttermilk.

5. Add ⅓ of the dry ingredients to the butter mixture while the mixer is running. When it is fully combined, add ⅓ of the wet ingredients and well. Continue, alternating wet and dry ingredients. Scrape the botto the bowl and mix for an additional 2 to 3 minutes.

6. Rub the butter on the bottom and sides of your skillet. Pour the batte the skillet and bake for 30 to 35 minutes, until cooked through.

7. While the cake is baking, make the icing by combining the butter, ha spread, sugar, and vanilla in the bowl of a stand mixer, or in a bowl w hand mixer. Whip, slowly, adding the heavy cream to combine. Chill.

8. When the cake is done, let it cool to room temperature before icing. Spread the icing evenly over the top of the cake and serve.

> Substitution tip: If hazelnut flavor is not your thing, you can replace the hazelnut spread with peanut butter for a twist!

Buttermilk Pound Cake with Blackberry Jam

VEGETARIAN

I love the concept behind pound cake: Let's take a pound of butter, a pound of sugar, and a pound of flour and see what happens! Lucky for us, it makes a delicious cake that is spongy, moist, and very buttery. It's as solid a cake ratio as there is.

SERVES 6 TO 8

PREP TIME: 20 MINUTES

COOK TIME: 1 HOUR 15 MINUTES

FOR THE CAKE

1 pound butter, plus more for greasing

1 teaspoon vanilla extract

2½ cups granulated sugar

6 eggs

3½ cups cake flour

2 teaspoons baking powder

1 teaspoon sea salt

¼ teaspoon mace

1 cup buttermilk

FOR THE JAM

2 cups fresh blackberries

1 tablespoon sugar

Juice of 1 lemon

1. Heat the oven to 325°F.

2. In the bowl of a stand mixer, or in a bowl with a hand mixer, cream th butter until light and fluffy. Add the vanilla and sugar, and continue be Beat in the eggs, one at a time.

3. In a large mixing bowl, sift the flour, baking powder, salt, and mace. again.

4. Add ⅓ of the dry ingredients to the wet ingredients and fully incorpor Add ⅓ of the buttermilk and mix thoroughly. Repeat with the remaini ingredients, alternating dry ingredients and buttermilk.

5. Grease your skillet with butter and pour in the batter, smoothing to e distribute.

6. Bake for 1 hour and 15 minutes.

7. While the cake is baking, combine the blackberries, sugar, and lemo in a small saucepan. Simmer, stirring occasionally, until the blackber break down and a thick jam forms. Remove from the heat to cool.

8. Allow the cake to rest for 15 minutes out of the oven before turning it onto a plate. Top with the blackberry jam and serve warm.

Menu-planning tip: Leftover pound cake, toasted and slathered with butter, is one of life's rare treats.

Strawberry Skillet Cake

VEGETARIAN

The beginning of spring is the best time to enjoy strawberries. The first sweet berries of the season are a revelation, a reminder that life and beauty are returning. This cake works to glorify the strawberry, with its simple, light, not-too-sweet batter and strawberries.

SERVES 6 TO 8

PREP TIME: 10 MINUTES

COOK TIME: 40 MINUTES

1¼ sticks salted butter, room temperature, plus more for greasing

1 cup sugar

3 eggs

1 teaspoon vanilla extract

1½ cups all-purpose flour

1¼ teaspoons baking powder

¾ teaspoon baking soda

½ teaspoon sea salt

1 cup Greek yogurt

1 pound fresh strawberries, hulled and halved

1. Preheat the oven to 350°F.

2. In the bowl of a stand mixer, or in a bowl with a handheld mixer, crea butter and sugar. Add in the eggs, one at a time, followed by the van

3. In a separate bowl, combine the flour, baking powder, baking soda, a salt.

4. Add ⅓ of the dry ingredients to the wet ingredients, mixing until fully incorporated. Follow with ⅓ of the Greek yogurt. Repeat with the remaining dry ingredients and yogurt, alternating. Scrape the bottom bowl and mix for an additional 1 to 2 minutes.

5. Fold in the strawberries by hand.

6. Grease your skillet with butter and gently pour in the batter.

7. Bake for 35 to 40 minutes, or until cooked through and golden brown

Substitution tip: Try making this cake with blackberries or peaches!

Monster Skillet Cookie

VEGETARIAN

There's a market in my parents' small Outer Banks town that has some of my favorite prepared foods in the world. The chicken salad is heavenly, and the house-fried chips are a delight. Best of all, however, are the market's monster cookies. Monster cookies are bound together by oatmeal and peanut butter, making them naturally gluten-free, and stuffed with candy-coated chocolate pieces and chocolate chips. They're buttery and a little crumbly, and with a cast-iron skillet crisping up both the edges and bottom, this giant-size version is absolute perfection.

SERVES 6 TO 8
PREP TIME: 15 MINUTES
COOK TIME: 20 MINUTES

4 tablespoons butter, room temperature, plus more for greasing

¾ cup brown sugar

½ cup granulated sugar

2 eggs

1 cup peanut butter

½ teaspoon vanilla extract

1 teaspoon baking soda

¼ teaspoon sea salt

2 cups oats

½ cup candy-coated chocolates (I like M&M's brand)

¼ cup chocolate chips

1. Preheat the oven to 350°F.

2. In the bowl of a stand mixer, or in a bowl with a hand mixer, cream together the butter, brown sugar, and sugar. Beat in the eggs, one at time. Then beat in the peanut butter, vanilla, baking soda, and salt.

3. Add the oats to the mixture, then slow the mixer and add the M&Ms chocolate chips.

4. Grease your skillet and scrape the batter into it. Gently spread the ba so it is even.

5. Bake for 15 to 18 minutes, until cooked through and crisp around the edges.

6. Allow to cool before serving.

Menu-planning tip: Top with a few scoops of ice cream for an impressive party centerpiece!

Churros

VEGETARIAN → QUICK AND EASY

There is a coffee shop in my neighborhood owned by the two friendliest people I've ever met, Tammy and Juan. Their coffee (which they roast themselves), is wonderful, the food is all handmade and delicious, and the company is incredibly warm. Tammy also occasionally makes churros, and when I stumble in on churro day, it's like Christmas morning.

SERVES 2 TO 4
PREP TIME: 15 MINUTES
COOK TIME: 15 MINUTES

FOR THE BATTER

1 cup water

¾ stick butter

3 tablespoons granulated sugar

1 cup all-purpose flour

¼ teaspoon ground cinnamon

¼ teaspoon vanilla extract

3 eggs

1 cup peanut oil

FOR THE TOPPING

½ cup sugar

1 tablespoon ground cinnamon

1. In a medium saucepan over medium heat, combine the water, butter sugar. Add the flour, cinnamon, and vanilla, reduce the heat to low, a

use a wooden spoon to stir vigorously until a dough ball forms.

2. Remove from the heat and beat in the eggs, one at a time.

3. Allow the dough to rest for a few minutes, then scoop it into a pastry fitted with a ½" star-shaped tip.

4. In your skillet, heat the peanut oil over medium-high heat to 375°F.

5. Pipe the dough directly into the oil, cutting each churro off at 6".

6. Fry for 2 minutes per side, transfer to a rack to cool, and repeat with remaining dough.

7. In a medium mixing bowl, combine the sugar and cinnamon.

8. When the churros are cool enough to handle, roll them in the sugar a cinnamon.

9. Serve warm.

Menu-planning tip: Churros are especially delicious with a chocolate dipping sauce. Mix ½ cup of chocolate chips with ½ cup of scalded heavy cream. Whisk together with a pinch of cinnamon.

Apple Pie

VEGETARIAN

Apple pie is classic for a reason. It's a staple on every fall menu, when the apples are bursting with flavor. Baking it in a skillet ensures that the dough is crisp (nary a soggy bottom here!), and the presentation is lovely. You can even go a little crazy and experiment with some decorative dough work on top to make the perfect centerpiece for your October dinner party.

SERVES 6 TO 8

PREP TIME: 30 MINUTES

INACTIVE TIME: 1 HOUR

COOK TIME: 55 MINUTES

FOR THE CRUST

2½ cups all-purpose flour

¾ cup salted butter, cubed, plus more for greasing

3 tablespoons granulated sugar

¼ teaspoon sea salt

¼ cup cold water

1 egg, beaten

FOR THE FILLING

2 tablespoons salted butter

6 Honeycrisp or Pink Lady apples, skin left on, cored and sliced ½" thick

4 tablespoons packed light brown sugar

1 teaspoon ground cinnamon

1 teaspoon ground ginger

1 teaspoon vanilla extract

1. In a food processor, combine the flour, butter, sugar, and salt. Pulse the mixture is crumbled and resembles coarse cornmeal.

2. While pulsing, add the water, 1 tablespoon at a time, until a ball form Wrap the dough in plastic wrap and chill for 1 hour.

3. Preheat the oven to 350°F.

4. In your skillet, melt the butter over medium heat. Stir in the apples.

5. Add the brown sugar, cinnamon, ginger, and vanilla. Cook for 15 min stirring frequently. Transfer to a bowl.

6. Rinse out the skillet and grease with butter.

7. Divide the dough into two portions, one slightly larger than the other. floured work surface, roll out the larger dough portion into a 15" roun Press into the bottom and sides of the skillet.

8. Pour the apple filling into the skillet.

9. Roll out the second dough portion into a 13" round. Place it over the the skillet and crimp the top crust with the bottom crust to seal the ed

10. Cut 4 (4") slits in the top crust, starting from the center and heading t the edges of the skillet. Brush the crust with the beaten egg.

11. Bake for 35 to 40 minutes, until browned and bubbling.

12. Let cool for 5 to 10 minutes before serving.

Ingredient tip: Add a cup of shredded gouda cheese to the dough for a burst of savory flavor.

Chocolate Pecan Pie

VEGETARIAN

I am deeply devoted to many different types of pie, and in my heart, they all have a season or a holiday when they are indispensable. Blueberry pie for my July birthday, Vinegar Pie for early spring, Apple Pie for early fall, and Chocolate Pecan Pie for Thanksgiving. It's not the only Thanksgiving pie, of course, but it's essential.

SERVES 6 TO 8
PREP TIME: 25 MINUTES
INACTIVE TIME: 1 HOUR
COOK TIME: 30 MINUTES

FOR THE CRUST

1¼ cups all-purpose flour

½ cup salted butter

1 tablespoon granulated sugar

Pinch sea salt

¼ cup cold water

FOR THE FILLING

3 eggs

½ cup brown sugar

½ cup granulated sugar

¼ teaspoon salt

¾ cup corn syrup

1 stick butter, melted

1½ cups chopped pecans

1 cup mini chocolate chips

1. In a food processor or blender, combine the flour, butter, granulated and salt. Pulse until the mixture is crumbled and resembles coarse cornmeal.

2. While pulsing, add the water 1 tablespoon at a time until a ball forms Wrap the dough in plastic wrap and chill for 1 hour.

3. Preheat the oven to 350°F.

4. In a large bowl, beat the eggs, then add the brown sugar, sugar, salt, syrup, and butter. Whisk together well. Stir in the pecans.

5. Roll out the dough on a floured work surface to a 15" round. Press in bottom and sides of your skillet.

6. Sprinkle half the chocolate chips evenly over the bottom of the crust. half the filling (stirring just before pouring) to the skillet. Sprinkle on t remaining chocolate chips and top with the remaining filling.

7. Bake for 30 minutes. Let cool completely before serving.

Ingredient tip: Add ½ cup of bourbon to the pie filling for a Kentucky twist.

Berry Buckle

VEGETARIAN

My grandma, Bobbie, called this sort of dish a "mountain pie," and she made me one for my birthday every year. Usually it was a blueberry mountain pie, but occasionally it was mixed berry and sometimes even peach. Always it was served piping hot out of the oven with a scoop of ice cream. Every year, I take the time to make myself a mountain pie for my birthday because it's truly the perfect midsummer dessert. The cake batter bubbles up and envelopes the berries, and the butter gives everything crisp edges while also maintaining a gooey center. It's the only way I want to celebrate my birthday.

SERVES 4 TO 6
PREP TIME: 10 MINUTES
COOK TIME: 40 MINUTES

½ cup salted butter

1 cup all-purpose flour

½ cup sugar

1¼ teaspoons baking powder

1 teaspoon sea salt

¾ cup whole milk

1 teaspoon vanilla extract

1 cup fresh blueberries

1 cup fresh blackberries

1 cup fresh strawberries, hulled and quartered

1. Preheat the oven to 350°F.

2. Add the butter to your skillet, and place it in the warming oven to mel

3. In a medium bowl, mix the flour, sugar, baking powder, salt, milk, and vanilla until combined.

4. Remove the skillet from the oven and pour the batter over the melted butter. Do not mix!

5. In a small bowl, combine the blueberries, blackberries, and strawber Pour on top of the batter. Do not mix!

6. Bake for 40 minutes, until bubbling and cooked through.

Menu-planning tip: This should always be served with vanilla ice cream. I like to buy the vanilla bean Talenti gelato because it's so rich and creamy that just a small scoop is satisfying.

Vinegar Pie

VEGETARIAN

I fully accept that some of you will get hung up on the name of this pie and not trust me when I tell you just how lovely it is. Vinegar pie is a chess pie derivative, which means that the foundation is eggs, sugar, and butter. Instead of being the dominant flavor, the apple cider vinegar gives the pie a tang and allows the stars of the show to be the delicate spices and custardy texture.

SERVES 6 TO 8
PREP TIME: 30 MINUTES
INACTIVE TIME: 1 HOUR
COOK TIME: 45 MINUTES

FOR THE CRUST

2½ cups all-purpose flour

¾ cup salted butter, cubed, plus more for greasing

3 tablespoons granulated sugar

¼ teaspoon sea salt

¼ cup cold water

1 egg, beaten

FOR THE FILLING

1 cup sugar

½ cup brown sugar

2 tablespoons all-purpose flour

1 teaspoon ground ginger

1 teaspoon ground cinnamon

1 teaspoon ground nutmeg

1 teaspoon ground cardamom

5 eggs

1 stick butter, melted

¼ cup apple cider vinegar

1 teaspoon vanilla extract

1. In a food processor or blender, combine the flour, butter, sugar, and Pulse until the mixture is crumbled and resembles coarse cornmeal.

2. While pulsing, add the water 1 tablespoon at a time until a ball forms Wrap the dough in plastic wrap and chill for 1 hour.

3. Preheat the oven to 325°F.

4. In a medium mixing bowl, combine the sugar, brown sugar, flour, gin cinnamon, nutmeg, and cardamom and mix well. Beat in the eggs, o a time, then add the butter, vinegar, and vanilla.

5. Grease your skillet with butter.

6. Roll out the dough on a floured work surface to a 15" round. Press in bottom and sides of the skillet.

7. Pour the filling into the crust. Bake for 45 minutes, until the pie is bro and mostly set. Allow to cool and set completely before serving.

Menu-planning tip: This pie is best served at room temperature, so it's perfect to make a few hours in advance.

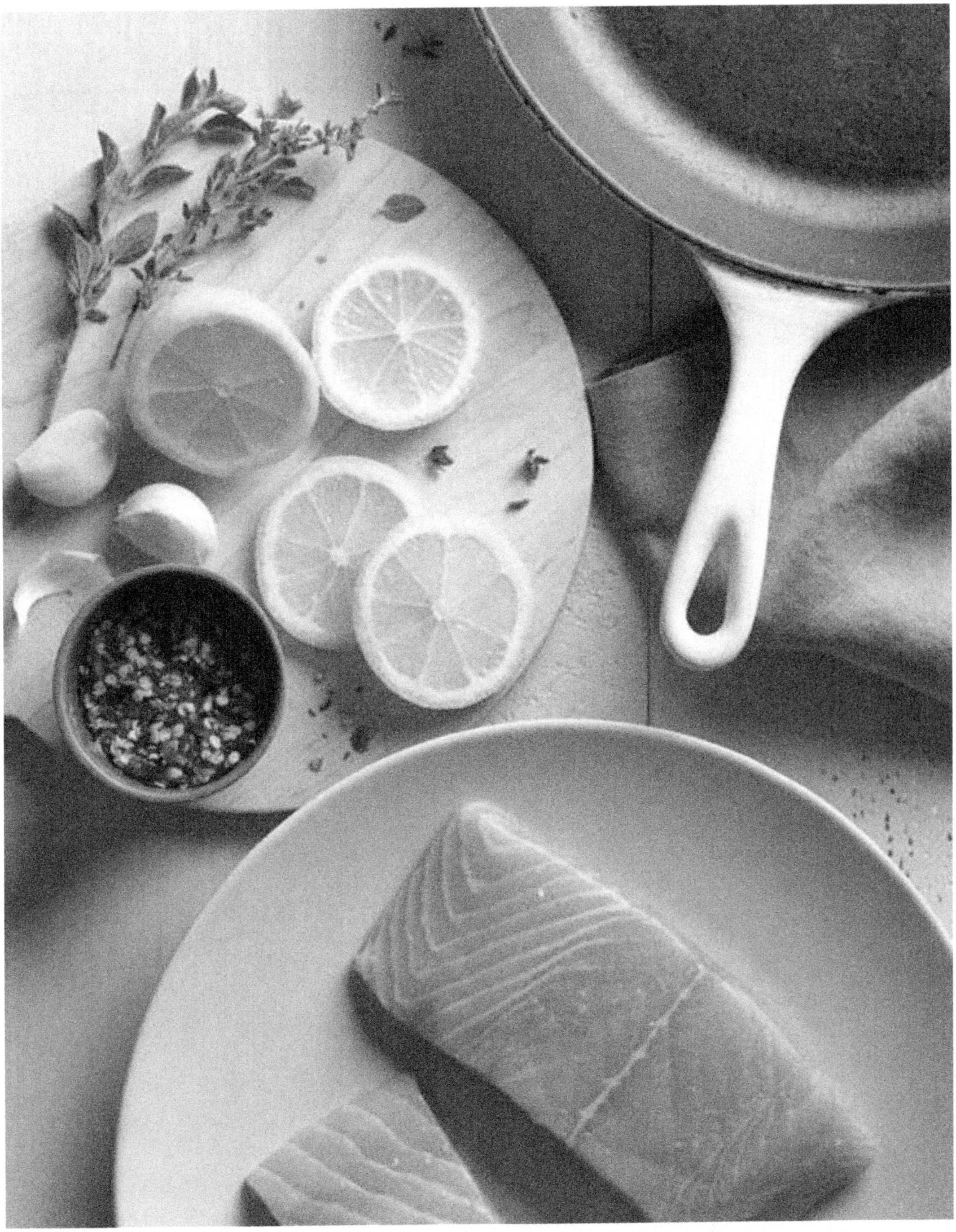

MEASUREMENT CONVERSIONS

VOLUME EQUIVALENTS (LIQUID)

US Standard	US Standard (ounces)	Metric (approximate)
2 tablespoons	1 fl. oz.	30 mL
¼ cup	2 fl. oz.	60 mL
½ cup	4 fl. oz.	120 mL
1 cup	8 fl. oz.	240 mL
1½ cups	12 fl. oz.	355 mL
2 cups or 1 pint	16 fl. oz.	475 mL
4 cups or 1 quart	32 fl. oz.	1 L
1 gallon	128 fl. oz.	4 L

VOLUME EQUIVALENTS (DRY)

US Standard	Metric (approximate)
⅛ teaspoon	0.5 mL
¼ teaspoon	1 mL
½ teaspoon	2 mL
¾ teaspoon	4 mL
1 teaspoon	5 mL
1 tablespoon	15 mL
¼ cup	59 mL
⅓ cup	79 mL
½ cup	118 mL
⅔ cup	156 mL
¾ cup	177 mL
1 cup	235 mL
2 cups or 1 pint	475 mL
3 cups	700 mL
4 cups or 1 quart	1 L

OVEN TEMPERATURES

Fahrenheit (F)	Celsius (C) (approximate)
250°F	120°C
300°F	150°C
325°F	165°C
350°F	180°C
375°F	190°C
400°F	200°C
425°F	220°C
450°F	230°C

WEIGHT EQUIVALENTS

US Standard	Metric (approximate)
½ ounce	15 g
1 ounce	30 g
2 ounces	60 g
4 ounces	115 g
8 ounces	225 g
12 ounces	340 g
16 ounces or 1 pound	455 g

Printed in Great Britain
by Amazon